Thistle

Thomas Kessenich

Published by
The Old Gypsum Printer, Inc. / Wings Publishing

Library of Congress Cataloging-In-Publication Data

ISBN 978-0-9771136-8-2

Copyright © 2009 by Thomas Kessenich

Publisher: The Old Gypsum Printer, Inc./Wings Publishing

Back cover drawing by Tyler Custer (Grandson) at an early age.

Printer: The Old Gypsum Printer, Inc.

To contact the author: nkessenich@bresnan.net

Printed in the United States of America

First Edition

July 2009

ACKNOWLEDGMENTS

Cia Fracchia of Ukiah, California. She proof read
the first few chapters of my book, always urging me on.

My wife, Nancy, and the family who
encouraged me to finish the book.

Phyllis Carpenter, of Grand Junction, Colorado,
for her constant input and proofing of the story.

Thank you my very special friend
Lavonne Gorsuch Of Grand Junction, Colorado.

Finally, to my daughter Julie Shedko, who took it upon herself
to act as my agent in an effort to bring all necessary
items together to get the story into publication.

I'm eternally grateful to all those who took interest
in my story and believed in me.

Dedication
To my Mom, Deloris Kessenich, whose unselfish lifestyle
during the hard times, enabled me to live my full life.

Chapter One

It would be another hot day in the town of Wheaton, Kansas, much like most days in this, the third straight year of draught. For Jake Ritter and his family the move west would be a welcome change, although leaving the town where you were born and raised isn't an easy thing to do. Neither is asking your children to give up their friends and the schools they attended all their lives.

It wasn't an easy choice to make for Jake, but when you lose your crop, your home, and the woman you've been married to for so many years, in the same fire, one has to believe it's time to move on and start over.

The tiny bell tinkled as Jake entered Wes Trimble's little grocery and hardware store. Lord knows, he must have heard that bell a thousand times while growing up on the family farm. His mother always made it a point to send Jake to pick up the mail and whatever groceries she needed every day, almost like she realized his dislike for farming. Of course, Jake loved coming to town on his bike as it gave him a chance to get away from his chores for a spell.

Wes had always been a good friend to the Ritter's down through the years. Jake still remembered the tractor Wes bought for his Pa during the Depression when their old "Iron Horse" gave up the ghost. Pa had three great harvest years in a row and was able to pay back every cent he owed Wes.

The sound of the bell alerted the owner of the store, and recognizing Jake, he took off his apron and came around to the customer side of the counter.

"Good morning Jake," he said as he greeted his old friend.

Jake shook the old man's hand as he bid him, "Good Morning". Wes detected that Jake was not his usual, flamboyant self.

"Something the matter my friend? The kids alright?"

"Nothing's the matter Wes. Is there somewhere we can talk in private?"

"Sure Jake. Sure."

He turned to the girl who was putting goods on the shelves and yelled to her to tend the store while he and Jake went to the back room.

"Oh Annie, would you bring in some coffee for our guest please?" She nodded and made her way behind the counter as the two men entered the room. The room was used mainly for storage; however, many was the time a wild poker game greeted the rising sun.

"Grab a chair my friend and sit down," urged Wes.

They sat across the table from one another as Annie entered the room with coffee and donuts. Wes leaned forward and spoke as he poured the coffee.

"You don't take cream or sugar do you Jake?"

"No," replied Jake, "black suits me just fine."

Neither man spoke as each selected a donut and sat back to enjoy their morning snack. Wes thought it very strange that his usually talkative friend was very somber on this day.

"Tell me Jake, how are the children doing? It's been six months now since the fire."

"Oh the kids are really doing well I guess," Jake replied.

He pulled a cigar from his pocket and unwrapped it and glancing over at Wes, asked if it would be alright if he smoked.

"Sure, my friend, you're welcome to smoke in here."

It was obvious that Jake was uneasy about something as he stood up and walked to the window and lit his cigar. Wes sat quietly sipping his coffee, not too sure what to say. Jake returned to the table and sat down.

"Josh is back playing baseball again. I've never seen a kid so wrapped up in sports, especially baseball, as he is," said Jake.

"Well he should be excited. The word around town is that Josh has great potential as a pitcher. They say, with the right coach, he'll be one of the finest pitchers in the state next year."

Jake was uneasy with what Wes was saying, not because he wasn't proud of his son's ability, but because he felt that Josh should be putting that energy to better use.

"Well, for my money," said Jake, "sports are just for dreamers. Look at how few actually make it to the big leagues. A kid puts all those hours into practice, urged on by some "has been" coach that keeps telling the boy he's another Walter Johnson . Then the day comes when he graduates and he finds out he really wasn't good enough to play at that level. Now he's faced with the question of what to do to make a living for the rest of his life."

"Come on Jake," pleaded Wes, "it's just a game to most kids and besides, it gives them something to do in their spare time."

"Yea, well running a farm is a twenty four hour job and a guy needs all the help he can get. Josh's away games and practices just double up the work load on me and the kids."

With that, Jake leaned back in his chair and took a long drag off his cigar as a smile appeared on his face.

"None of that matters any more anyway," said Jake, "because I've sold the farm, so the kids and I are heading for California."

"Oh no," gasped Wes, "you didn't sell the farm that has been in your family for nearly four generations?"

"Come on Wes," he pleaded, "don't make it any harder for me than what it already is. It's done and I can't go back now. With the sale of the farm and the insurance money from the fire, I've got a pretty good "nest egg.""

Wes studied his friend for a moment, remembering how unhappy Jake had always been, even as a boy, of having to work the land. It never suited him and probably never would.

"You never took to farming like your daddy, did you Jake? You always had to know what was further on down the road and around the corner."

It was evident to Jake that Wes was very upset with him but he felt it was more because they were such good friends. He felt he really owed Wes a better explanation so he chose his words very carefully.

"That's never been a secret Wes. When Pa died I felt obligated to keep the place going for Ma. Then I married Martha, and the children came along, and my obligations and responsibilities just got bigger and bigger. Well, Ma has passed on and Martha is gone and now it's just me and the kids, so for the first time in my life I'm going to do what I want to do."

Wes realized his friend had made up his mind but he wanted Jake to be aware of all the aspects of what he was planning to do.

"What about the children Jake?" Wes asked. "How do they feel about giving up their friends and changing schools? Just like you, this is the only home they've ever known."

A little upset that Wes was so against their going, he stood up and walked over to the window and looked out, not really wanting to look his long time friend in the eyes.

"Come on Wes," he begged, "you know it would be better for Beth if we got out of here. She doesn't even hold a decent conversation any more and if she doesn't snap out of it she's going to fail at school. Seeing the house burn down with her mother inside has really affected her."

Wes was very surprised to learn about the girl's problems and decided to let up on Jake and not upset him further.

"Does Doc think she will be alright as time goes by?"

"He thinks she will some day, all in her own time. There's nothing physically wrong with her, it's just a mental block and it's only a matter of time before she returns to normal."

Wes got up from his chair and walked over to Jake to reassure his friend that, no matter what happens, he would be there for him and the family.

"How's Little Jake holding up? Pretty big happenings for a little boy his age," asked Wes.

"Well you know what they say about him, Wes? Little Jake is Little Jake. For a little guy, he seems to be bouncing back better than the rest of us. You know, when I told him his Mother died, the only thing he asked me was where she had gone to? When I told him she had gone to Heaven he just looked at me, wiped his eyes, gave me a hug and said he'd miss her."

Wes gave a little chuckle and said, "You're right about him Jake, he seems to figure things out quickly."

Jake was tired of having to defend his position to Wes and besides, he was taking up too much of Wes' time.

"Well Wes," said Jake, "other than saying good-bye, I wanted to make sure my debt with you is taken care of before the kids and I leave in the morning."

Wes, realizing there was nothing more he could say that would change Jake's mind, walked to the door and asked Molly to get Jake's bill.

"Well Jake, it won't be the same around here without you and the family, but I know how you feel, so I won't try to change your mind."

Jake was visibly relieved the conversation had shifted to his plans for moving on and he answered in an upbeat tone, one of excitement and expectation.

"First thing this morning, I went over to Les Bingham's and bought that '39 station wagon he had for sale. Could have gotten a new one, I guess, but I wanted to get going right away. It'll get us there alright and then I'll trade it in on a new one. We'll get packed and hit the road at first morning light. No sense putting it off any longer."

Molly handed Wes the bill and Wes looked it over to make sure it was in order.

"It comes to $210.00 Jake," he said as he handed the bill to his friend.

Jake thumbed through his wallet and pulled out two one hundred dollar bills and a ten and handed them to Wes.

"You know my friend," said Jake in a somber tone, "can't thank you enough for all your kindnesses, not only for now, but for all the years we've known you. God knows, a friend like you comes along but once in a lifetime."

He took a step toward Wes and extended his hand.

"I'll miss you Wes Trembel,"he said softly.

"I'll miss you too, my friend. You know where I am so keep in touch."

The two men walked to the outer door and Wes opened it for Jake. He looked up as the little bell tinkled, hesitated and then walked onto the sidewalk. He made his way up the street without looking back.

Ж

The White Dove café had its usual amount of coffee drinkers and gossipers on hand to get the day going. Of course, the ceiling fans going full blast, helped to bring in the town folks, especially when the morning temperature was so high.

An unusual amount of truckers, who were hauling supplies to the Army base, made for a busy breakfast for the two waitresses and one cook. The older of the two women was Ethyl. She didn't move very fast but she had been there so long it was commonplace to just wait her out in a good natured fashion. She had only one speed but when you own the place, such as she did, that was good enough.

The younger waitress was Maggie Trask, out of high school for a couple of years now, doing the same job she started the day she graduated tending tables. She had two older brothers, no longer living at home, who worked at the grain sheds. When you lived in Wheaton the only jobs that weren't farming were in the small businesses or the grain sheds.

Maggie lived at home with three younger sisters, a mother who rarely left the house and a drunkard father who worked in the garage at the gas station when he was sober. Maggie, being the oldest daughter, was expected to take care of the younger children when she wasn't working. She did the wash, the cooking of the evening meals and the general upkeep of her younger sisters. The only contribution her mother made was to complain about her aches and pains and how tired she always got when she helped with the dishes which she did on occasion.

Maggie thought it was a wonder her Ma ever got out of bed, considering the number of children she had given birth to. Working at the café and then tending to the family made for some long days for Maggie. She had learned to accept the hard work but she knew she could never accept her father's violent temper whenever he drank. She never could understand why a man's hands became so free when he drank.

"Ya got one up Maggie," yelled the cook.

"Be right there Artie, soon as I fill these cups", she yelled back. Two truckers at one of the tables were kidding around with her, as most truckers tended to do, as she had a great sense of humor.

"Say Maggie," one began, "why doesn't a pretty young thing like you give up this table hopp'in and take up with a good look'n old boy like me? We could see a lot of country together."

Maggie had learned all the come-backs as she said, "Now Amos, if it's a choice between riding in your hot, old, sweaty truck or waiting tables in here, where it's really cool, then I'm taking the café."

The locals chuckled as she made her way back behind the counter where she picked up the "ham and over easy" and sat the plate down in front of Sheriff Manson. She reached back and grabbed the coffee pot and was doing refills as Jake walked in and seated himself on the stool next to the sheriff.

"Mornin' Maggie. Mornin' sheriff," he greeted.

"Good morning Jake," answered the sheriff, never bothering to look up or stop eating.

"Good morning Jake," said Maggie." What can I get for you this morning?"

Jake scanned the menu, put it back in the rack and said, "I don't know why I even look in the damn thing, it never changes. Just give me a donut and a cup of coffee."

Sheriff Manson looked over at Jake, who withdrew a cigar from his shirt pocket and was about to light it.

"Damn it Jake," he yelled, "you know I can't stand cigar smoke when I'm eating."

"Oh sorry sheriff," Jake said, "I forgot about that."

"Well don't be forgettin' it," he grumbled, "you know that irritates the Hell out of me."

Maggie sat the plate with the donut on it in front of Jake and as he broke it in half and dunked part of it into his coffee she asked him a question.

"Say Jake, how come you're all dressed up on a work day? Going over to Topeka on business or something?"

"Nope," he answered as he continued to dunk the other half of the donut, "just paying up the people I owe and getting ready to pull out of this "Dust Bowl" of a town."

It shocked Maggie to hear him say that he and the family were thinking of leaving Wheaton. She had watched Jake's children when they were little and all of them were very close friends. In reality, the Ritter family were her best friends and the thought of losing them really bothered her. She was lost for words as she blurted out, "What do you mean pull out? You don't even have a decent car to drive."

"Oh yes I do," he answered as he swung around on his stool and pointed out the window at his newly acquired station wagon parked across the street.

"Took ole man Benjamin's wagon off his hands, cash money."

He swung back around facing the counter and, in a proud voice, addressed the sheriff once again.

"Ain't she a looker sheriff?"

The sheriff looked out the window at the car and then at Jake and answered.

"If you're talking about Maggie, then yes. If you're talking about that junk heap across the street, then no."

"Com'on sheriff," Jake pleaded. "She's got a few good trips left in her, don't you think?"

The sheriff stood up, put his money for the bill on the counter, placed a toothpick in his mouth and placed his hand on Jake's shoulder.

"Jake," he replied, "the only trip that junk heap is going to make is back to the junk yard."

As the sheriff made his way to the door, Jake relit his cigar and yelled after him, "You'll see sheriff. That car's going to get us all the way to California."

The sheriff laughed as he closed the door behind him. Jake spun his stool back around to face the counter and took another sip of coffee.

He looked over at Maggie and said, "What the Hell does he know about cars anyway? All he ever does is hide on the side street and look for speeders to come by."

Maggie wasn't interested in what the sheriff was doing, but rather about the statement Jake made about leaving.

"What do you mean you're going to California?"

"Just what I said darlin'. The kids and I are heading west where the jobs are plentiful in those airplane factories. I hear they're crying for workers to build all the planes and tanks for our troops", he answered.

"But what about the farm and the schooling for the kids? Don't they have a say in all this?"

"Yep, they do. After hearing all they had to say, I decided that we were going to California," answered Jake.

She couldn't believe what she was hearing. The children loved it in Wheaton and all their friends were here and there was no reason for them to want to leave.

"I can't believe they all agreed to go Jake," she countered.

"Oh, none of them wanted to go but the last say in this family is mine, so we're going, like it or not."

Maggie was visibly upset with the situation. She glared at Jake, threw her towel down on the counter and retreated to the kitchen where she sobbed quietly. After a few minutes she pulled herself together and returned to the counter. Why should she care if the Ritters move away, she thought to herself. Just because she had watched the children over the years and just because Jake had always treated her well, doesn't mean she had any hold on them. Having gained her composure, she refilled Jake's coffee cup.

"So you've made up your mind and you're leaving?" she asked in a very serious tone.

Jake put his hand on hers. He looked up at her and spoke softly.

"Come on Maggie, don't make it any harder for me than it already is."

She leaned forward and spoke softly so no one else could hear.

"Jake, you're the only man in this whole damn town who ever gave a hoot if things were alright for me. What am I supposed to be, happy?"

Jake threw his hands into the air and gave out with a knowing smile.

"Well Hell Maggie, you're free, white and twenty-one so why don't you come with us?"

"You know I can't do that. Who would tend to my sisters if I just picked up and left?"

"One thing about it Maggie, they're not your kids and most of all they are not your responsibility."

Her face reddened as she was quick to reply.

"Well, what do you know about anything anyway?"

Jake had waited a long time to answer that question and jumped at the chance to express his opinion.

"I know if you dedicate yourself to your sisters, you'll only get slapped around by your father. Some day, when he really ties one on and comes home stupid drunk, you could end up dead. Just as bad as that, you'll tend tables for someone else all your life and you'll never

9

have anything for yourself."

Maggie turned slightly so she wasn't looking him straight in the face. "What would people say if I went runnin' off that way, with you being a family man and all?"

Jake got to his feet, lay down the money for the tab and gave her a long look.

"I didn't ask you to go to bed with me Maggie. I only offered you a ride out of this God forsaken town, with a chance to do what's in your heart to do. I'll drive by your house on our way out so you and the kids can say your good-bys. All I ask is that you think on it for awhile."

Maggie started to answer but Jake wheeled around and crossed the room toward the door. She stood there watching as he opened the door and looked back at her.

"Just think about it. That's all I ask."

Ж

It had been a long, hard day for Maggie at the café, making the long walk home even more unbearable in the heat. She couldn't get Jake, and what he had said, out if her mind. He had stirred up thoughts inside of her she had never, ever, contemplated before today. Oh sure, she had thought about getting a place of her own, like her brothers did after they graduated, but never gave the idea of moving away any consideration at all.

She picked the leaves from the bushes as she strolled up the path leading to the house. She knew she had deep feelings for her sisters and couldn't just pick up and leave without a good reason. She also knew, deep down, her father was giving her reason enough with his drunkenness and the ease at which he slapped her and her sisters around.

She reached the stairs and climbed to the top of the porch and turned to take one last look toward town. "Is Jake right," she thought? "Was there no future for her in Wheaton waiting on tables and taking care of her sisters?"

She let out a big sigh as she opened the door and went inside.

"Maggie, you're home," yelled Lottie, the oldest of her younger sisters.

"Hi Lottie, where are Tracy and Kim?"

"They're in the bathtub," she replied. "They got filthy dirty playing in Papa's old car, and did Mama get mad."

Maggie took Lottie by the hand and walked toward the bathroom.

"Come on. Let's go see how they're doing," Maggie said with a smile on her face.

From the back bedroom came her mother's voice, yelling, "Is that you Maggie?"

"It's me Ma", Maggie yelled back.

"Well it's about time. Where have you been anyway, you're a half hour late?"

"I'm sorry Ma, I had to wait for Verna to get there. She was a half hour late again."

Maggie entered the bathroom where the two youngest were having a grand time playing in the tub. Kim, the youngest, was glad to see her older sister and Maggie greeted her with a smile and a big "Hello." Tracy, one year older than Kim, had a frown on her face and hung her head and in a whisper said, "Hi sis."

Maggie knew her sisters were told not to play around the old car that sat in the field.

"Hey you two, who said you could play in the old car? If Papa finds out he'll skin you both alive."

Kim, still smiling, answered, "We were playing "bus" and I drove all the way to St. Louis and Tracy drove all the way home. It was so much fun Maggie."

Tracy wasn't as thrilled with the situation because she got a swat across the behind with the belt for taking Kim down to the car. Maggie reached down and lifted Tracy from the tub, who immediately threw her arms around Maggie's neck and began to cry.

Maggie tossed a towel around Tracy and began to dry her off. Tracy continued to cry, which was unusual for her.

"Hey sis, what's the matter? It's not like you to carry on so," Maggie asked.

Tracy pulled away from Maggie and turned her naked body around so her older sister could see the welt on her hip. Maggie knew very well how the welt got there. Her mother always used a strap on

11

the kids when they did something wrong, especially if she had to get out of bed to "Straighten those kids out," as she put it.

"It hurts Maggie," her sister complained.

"I know sweetheart. Let me dry you off and then we'll put some salve on it, ok?"

Lottie dried Kim and they all went into the bedroom to get clean clothes. Maggie applied salve to Tracy's bruise and when both were dressed she sent them out to play in the front yard, warning them about staying away from the shed and the car. Maggie straightened up the living room before entering her mother's bedroom. She knocked lightly on the door frame as she spoke. "Are you awake Ma?"

"What else can I be with those confounded kids runnin' around screaming all the time?"

"Ma, I need to talk to you about something."

"Can't it wait Maggie? I have a splitting headache right now."

"It's real important Ma and I need to ask you before Pa gets home."

Her mother sat up and swung her legs over the side of the bed and sat there looking down at the floor.

"Go ahead," she urged, "I can see you won't take no for an answer. What is it that's so damn important anyway?"

Maggie sat beside her on the bed but was a little hesitant to speak. However, she realized the importance of what she wanted to say, so she began.

"Ma, would it be alright if I found a place of my own to live?" Before she could elaborate on the subject her mother began to yell.

"Are you crazy? You know your Pa won't let you do that. Who'll take care of the kids and do the cooking?"

"But Ma," she pleaded, "the boys moved out right after they graduated and no one said anything. I've been helping out for three years now and I want a life of my own."

Her mother got to off the bed and walked over to a small table and poured herself a shot of whiskey. Maggie joined her mother at the table and placed her hand on her shoulder.

"Come on Ma, do you have to drink so much? It's going to kill you some day."

She reached to take the glass out of her hand but her mother shoved her away.

"Get away from me. What do you know anyway? You come in here and tell me you want to move out when you know I can hardly get around anymore."

"But Ma-------."

"Don't you 'but me', young lady. You know damn well we need you here at home. It's your duty to look after me and your Pa and your sisters."

Maggie was riled now as she stood face to face with her mother and began yelling back.

"What do you mean it's my duty? You're just taking your responsibility and dumping it off onto me. You want me to feel guilty about leaving the kids. Well it's not going to work, Ma. They're your kids. You had them and you and Pa can take care of them."

Maggie was stunned by the force of the slap her mother laid across her face as she reeled back across the bed. Her mother lunged at her screaming. Maggie slapped the glass from her mother's hand and it slammed against the wall spilling the booze onto the rug.

"That's just about all the thanks I get around here Ma. You can call me what you want, but why don't you look into the mirror some day and see the drunkard you've become?"

Her mother braced herself against the table as Maggie continued.

"You and Pa are just alike. You sure had fun having all of us but neither of you want anything to do with raising us."

Maggie slammed the door so hard on her way out of the bedroom that two pictures fell onto the floor. She made her way to her own room crying, and once inside, locked the door. She could hear her mother yelling from across the hall.

"You ungrateful little bitch. Wait until your father gets home, he'll tan your ass good for ya."

She returned to her room and slammed the door as hard as Maggie had, causing yet another picture to fall to the floor. Maggie lay across her bed, crying. Oh my God, she thought, what had she done? Her Pa would beat her to within an inch of her life when he found out. After a while she stopped crying and fell asleep.

Chapter Two

The morning sun began its assent into another cloudless sky bringing with it a promise of yet another unbearably hot day for the people of Wheaton, Kansas. The heat of the day didn't seem to matter to the Ritter family for, on this day, they would load up the newly acquired station wagon and head for California, bringing with them the hopes and dreams of a new life and a new beginning.

Beth was being pushed on the old tire swing by her friend, Jimmy Brant, who had come by from a neighboring farm to say good-by. Beth and Jimmy had been close friends all through grade school and into her first year of high school. Now, with the upcoming move to California, all their dreams of graduating together were slowly becoming a thing of the past.

"How come your Pa wants to move to California and take you away from the only home you've ever known?"

Beth seemed to take forever to answer, as she just seemed to be in a trance, watching the earth beneath her go round and round.

"I really don't know why we are going, Jimmy", she answered.

"None of it makes any sense to me any more. In a way, I'm glad we're leaving this farm."

Her voice went to a whisper. "I lost my mother here", she said as she began to sob.

Jake looked up from his task of loading the car for their journey and saw Beth and Jimmy at the swing.

"Come on Beth." he yelled, "It's time to get moving."

Jimmy slowed the swing and Beth touched her feet to the ground and stood up. She turned and faced her friend, and as they held hands, Beth kissed him on the cheek. The kiss took him by surprise and before he could react she turned and ran down the pathway to where the family was waiting for her. Beth turned and waved to him as he yelled, "Good-by."

Jake sent the kids back into what was left of the house to bring out the final belongings to be taken with them. Part of the kitchen and the back room is all that remained now and it was in here their belongings were stored.

"Josh," yelled Jake, "bring me those boxes so I can tie them to the rack."

Josh sat the boxes down by his father's side, and as Jake fit each one onto the rack, Josh touched his father's arm.

"Pa, he said softly, do you think we're doing the right thing by leaving here?"

Jake didn't answer the question as he tied the ropes to secure the boxes. As he tugged on the ropes, in one final effort to make sure all was secure, he gave Josh final instructions.

"Josh," he commanded, "you go back to the house and make sure we've got everything. You make sure now because once we're on the road there's no coming back for anything."

"But Pa," Josh began.

"No buts son. Just do as I tell you."

Josh looked into his father's eyes, hoping for some assurance that everything would be alright. When it wasn't forthcoming, he turned and made his way toward the house.

Jake leaned on the car and scanned the horizon as he wiped the sweat from inside his hat. He knew, for himself, it would be a great day, a day in which he could finally put behind him all the sorrow and anguish of a tragedy that would haunt him forever. Relocating was a gamble and he knew it, but with Sarah gone, the farm held no meaning for him any longer.

It seemed like everything he ever did, since he could remember, he did because someone else wanted him to. Like most fathers, Jake's dad always believed the most important thing a father could do for his family would be to have a farm which would be passed down from generation to generation.

His mother, however, saw an unusual dislike for farming in her son and always knew he kept inside him the yearning to see what lie over the mountains to the West. Before Jake could realize that dream, his father died, leaving him with the responsibility of caring for his mother. This, of course, meant running the farm in his father's place. Then he married Sarah and with the arrival of three children over the years the farm continued to be their salvation and a way of life.

Now, however, with the death of Sarah, only one year after his mother passed on, and the charred remains of the only home he ever knew, he finally realized his chance to see what was on the other side of the mountains to the West. He had made up his mind to try something new, something for himself and his children, an opportunity that may never come their way again.

Jake heard the children coming and as he watched them come across the yard for the last time, he pulled a cigar from his shirt and lit it. He had a habit of smoking a cigar when an uncomfortable situation arose that demanded some serious thought, when the moment of truth was at hand.

"The house is empty Pa," he reported. "The only things left are Little Jake's bicycle and Beth's old doll house you built for her on her fifth birthday."

The three children stood together in front of their father, waiting for some clue as to the fate of their prized possessions and they each held out hope there would be room for them somewhere in or on the car.

"Look kids," Jake explained, "there just isn't enough room for everything."

When he began talking, the children were looking into his eyes, but after his announcement the children had focused their eyes toward the ground at their feet. Jake knelt down in front of his youngest son and tried to make eye contact.

"Look son," Jake began, "I promise to get you a new bike when we get to where we are going, only this time we'll get a Schwinn, a new red one with a light on the front and a bell. What do you say, partner, is it a deal?"

A smile crossed Little Jake's face as he looked into his father's eyes and blurted out, "It's a deal Pa."

With that, Jake hugged the boy, not only as a gesture of thanking him, but to buy himself a little more time before he had to confront Beth about her doll house. She was still looking at the ground, her hands folded in front of her. Jake, still kneeling, put her hands in his and gave them a little tug. Beth, with tears in her eyes, looked away. Jake gently tugged on her hands once more.

"Look at me Beth. Please look at me," he pleaded.

She slowly turned her head toward her father and as tears made their way down her cheeks, she looked into his eyes. When he saw the tears, he hesitated and looked down at the ground, trying to find the right words to say. He looked up at her once more as the boys stood motionless.

"Please try to understand honey," he pleaded, "there's only enough room for important things. Besides, you're bigger now and you hardly ever play with your dolls any more."

Jake looked for some sign of understanding on her part but there was no indication she would agree with him. She merely turned and looked at his stuffed chair, securely tied to the car.

Without turning to look, Jake knew what she was looking at. He stood up, still with her hands in his, and as their eyes met he knew he was defeated. Through her tears he sensed the hurt and sorrow his daughter had endured. She, more than anyone, had suffered the most, so much so she hadn't spoken much since the fire. Her mother had used the doll house as a learning tool to teach Beth about caring for a home for a few years. They had made little curtains for the windows and, when there was a little extra money, they would go to town and buy tiny pieces of toy furniture for the rooms. The big house had burned down and the only link to her mother was the little house they kept together.

Jake motioned to his son Josh to join him at his side, which he quickly did.

"Yes sir?"

"Unload my chair and tie your sister's doll house in its place on the car," Jake ordered.

"You bet Pa," Josh answered as he hoisted the doll house onto his shoulder and headed for the car.

Beth put her arms around her father and, in a whisper, thanked him.

Jake patted her on the back and looked over at Little Jake, standing there with a big grin on his face. Jake put the cigar back into his mouth.

"Well," he ordered in a gruff tone, "don't just stand there smiling, let's hit the road."

Little Jake let out a big "hurrah" as they all took their places inside the car. Jake gave the load one last look and couldn't help but believe people would mistake them for Okies. What the Hell, he said to himself, who cares, we're on our way.

Jake squeezed in behind the wheel of the car and gently turned the key on. The four of them sat in silence as the car slowly made its way down the driveway. Each wanted one last look at the only home they had ever known. Down the old dusty road past the huge 'weeping willow' tree which supported the two ropes tied to an old tire they all swung on for so many years. The car came to a stop at the end of the lane. There, the rusty old mailbox stood with its strands of 'Virginia Creeper' twined around the post and over the box.

It had always been one of Sarah's favorite things on the farm, always lamenting about its announcement of the changing season. In the warmth of summer, it was a brilliant green, but with the first hint of winter's frost, it turned a brilliant red while waiting for the first snow.

For a brief moment, Jake hesitated from entering the highway. Josh felt the uncertainty his father was displaying. He placed his hand on Jakes shoulder from the back seat.

"We better get going," he urged, "we have a long way to go."

"You're right son," Jake answered, "thank you."

As the car made its way onto the main road, each took that last look back, each keeping their inner most feelings to themselves. As the homestead faded from view, all eyes focused on the road ahead. In the deafening sound of silence, each wondered what was waiting for them around the next bend in the road. Jake never looked back.

Ж

That same morning sun was not a welcome sight for Maggie as she desperately struggled to get out of bed. She hurt terribly from the beating her drunken father had given her the night before. Her mother had told him of their argument and, much worse, about her desire to find a place of her own. He used a belt this time and Maggie was bruised on her arms and legs. Her face was cut above her left eye which, very quickly, turned an ugly purple color.

She sat on the end of her bed and tried to assess her situation. She had begun to dress herself when Lottie quietly entered the room and stood before her big sister. Lottie was twelve now and understood

18

what was going on between the girls and her father.

"Maggie," she said, "I heard what you told Pa about wanting to get a place of your own. The girls and I agree that you should go."

Maggie replied quickly, "I can't do that Lottie. Who would watch out for the three of you?"

"We're alright Maggie," she assured her sister.

"Pa only spanks us now and then, not like what he does to you."

Maggie placed her head in her hands and softly told her sister she didn't know what to do.

Lottie helped her sister to her feet and led her to the dresser and instructed her to look into the mirror. Maggie steadied herself on the front of the dresser.

"I don't want to look in the mirror," she answered.

Lottie placed her hand under her sister's chin and gently forced her head upward.

"Look what he's done to you Maggie."

Maggie looked for a brief moment at her battered image in the mirror and sank heavily into the chair by the dresser. With her hands covering her face, she wept softly.

"What can I do Lottie? What on earth am I going to do?"

Lottie went quickly to the bed and retrieved a bag full of clothes and returned to her sister's side.

"I've packed some of your things in this bag. It's enough to get you by until you get on your feet again.

Maggie had a look of doubt and surprise on her face as she looked her sister in the eyes.

"I can't do that Lottie. I can't just leave all of you here by yourselves."

"You were right Maggie, we're not your responsibility. We know you love us and we love you too but it's time for you to live your own life. Besides, we don't want to ever see you like this again."

The quiet tones that held their conversations were shattered by a loud, angry yell from their father from the kitchen.

"Maggie, why aren't you out here fixin' breakfast?"

The girls could hear his footsteps coming down the hall toward the bedroom.

"Quick Maggie," urged Lottie, "go to the door while I hide the bag of clothes under the bed."

Maggie opened the door at the same time her father kicked it with his foot.

"Well you are up," he said in a sarcastic tone of voice.

Without looking at her, he spun around and returned to the kitchen where he seated himself at the table. Maggie followed him into the kitchen and put on her apron as she looked out the window. She turned and faced her father.

"What is it you want for breakfast?"

He looked up as if to answer and for the first time saw her face. Like most drinkers, who become violent and beat their family members, he couldn't remember what had happened. However, deep down, he knew he was the cause of her grief.

"Oh my God", he said to himself.

Maggie walked over to him at the table, somehow unafraid of him now and stood over him.

"Take a good look Pa. Not a very pretty sight is it?"

He just sat there and said nothing, trying to recall what drove him to hurt his daughter so. He could stand her glare no more and turned away in silence. Realizing her father was not going to answer her question, she returned to the stove and turned to face him again.

"I'm going to fix breakfast for everyone and then I'm leaving this house for good," she announced in a loud voice.

Now he remembered the argument he had had with her the night before and his temper surfaced once again.

"Like Hell you are," he yelled as he stood up and faced her.

"The Hell I'm not," she screamed back at him.

He took a step toward her as she grabbed the butcher knife from the drain board and held it with two hands in front of her as if for protection.

"You hit me again Pa and I'll make sure you don't have any more kids," she warned as she backed away from him.

He stopped where he was and pointed a finger at her and his words grew louder and more demanding.

"Put down that fool knife before someone gets hurt."

"No Pa, not this time." She answered quickly and with authority and a sense of urgency in her voice.

"You've hurt me for the last time and I don't want you to ever hit me again," she screamed.

The argument was so heated, neither of them heard the car drive up to the front of the house. From where Jake was parked, it was easy to hear all the screaming and yelling going on inside the house. He honked the horn twice to announce their arrival. Josh made a move to get out of the car but Jake grabbed him by the arm.

"Where you goin' boy?"

"Maggie's in trouble Pa and we've got to help her."

"Not this time," Jake demanded.

"But Pa………..

"No buts Josh," Jake insisted. "This is their home, their argument and their property."

Josh closed the door as Jake gave the horn three more quick blasts. Inside the house Maggie heard the horn and took a quick glance out of the window.

"Who be a call'en this time of the morning?" the old man asked.

"It's the Ritter family," she replied, "they're heading for California and they've come to say good-by."

"Well, you're not going out there looking like that," he insisted.

"I'm going out there Pa and you're not going to stop me," she yelled back.

He lunged at her as she dashed through the doorway leading out of the kitchen into the yard. She slammed the door just as her father reached the doorway and the force of the door knocked him backward onto the floor. He reached up in pain as he put both hands on his face, He was bleeding from his nose, which had been broken. His moment of anguish had given Maggie time to run to the car.

"You're a mess Maggie. What the hell is going on here?" Jake asked.

"No time to explain. Can I still go with you?"

"Hell yes," Jake answered, "get in."

As she ran around the car to the passenger side, her father burst onto the porch with a shotgun in his hands. He fired off one shot that caught a tree limb above the car, bringing down a flurry of leaves and twigs.

"Hurry Jake," she yelled frantically, "go around the back way before he reloads."

Jake gunned the engine and peeled out on the soft dirt, spewing dust and gravel everywhere. As they went by the back door of the house, Lottie came running out carrying the bag she had packed for Maggie.

"Maggie, Maggie!!" she yelled as she ran along side of the car. "Here's your bag."

Jake slammed on the brakes as Lottie threw the bag through the open car window.

"Get out of the way Lottie," the old man yelled as he took aim at the car from the back porch.

Lottie refused to move as Jake gunned it again and sped toward the main road.

"Get down Lottie," Maggie yelled, leaning out of the car door.

Lottie fell face first onto the ground as one last shot rang out. Chicken feathers and dust flew everywhere as the old man pulled his shot downward and to the right, not wanting to hit his daughter.

Lottie sat up as she watched the car turn onto the main road and pick up speed. As she brushed the hair from her eyes and the dust from her clothes, she said in a whisper, "I love you Maggie. I love you."

Chapter Three

So it was then, the stage was set for these five adventurers, thrown together by separate tragedies. Of course for Jake, his dreams for something better was now a reality, a chance to cast his lot, like all dreamers, into the fantasies of the unknown. He had always believed there was something better out there than Wheaton, Kansas had to offer.

For the children, however, it was a matter of placing their hopes on their father's dreams, always believing he would show them the way to fulfilling their own dreams. A kind of blind love that tells you everything will be alright because he's your father.

Maggie, of course, was torn between her guilt of leaving her sisters in an awful environment and her belief that there was someone, somewhere, who could love her and give her the kind of life most girls dream about. She knew, deep down the guilt she felt would have to be suppressed because there was no going back now. She had finally stood up to her father and made her choice.

Of course, Maggie and the children knew full well their futures were riding on the confidence and brashness of Jake. As questionable as that may have seemed to them, there was no doubt in Jakes mind he could accomplish anything he set his mind to. This was his moment. This was his dream and he was going to make it happen. The others prayed to God he was right.

They had made their way westward after reaching Nebraska and had stopped for the night at "Dick Lingo Auto Court". It was built somewhat like a fort, with the cabins forming the outside wall and six garages facing each other in the middle. Dick Lingo was also the cook in the café up front and was famous for his hamburgers.

Jake was the first to waken. He opened his eyes and looked around an unfamiliar room, trying to recall the events that brought him to this place.

A smile crossed his face as he bounded out of bed and onto the boys bed where he began jumping up and down to waken them up. "Rise and shine you lazy bums." he yelled, "We've got a long way to go today."

Josh pulled the covers back over his head, as best he could, not really sharing his father's jovial mood so early in the morning.

"Come on Pa, it's barely daylight," he complained.

"Ya Pa, there's no school today," Little Jake chimed in.

Jake hopped off the bed and onto the floor where he began getting dressed. He looked over at the motionless boys in the other bed.

"Come on boys," he urged, "we've got a lot of miles to cover before we get to California."

He buckled his belt, put on his hat and headed for the door. He looked back at the boys sitting on the side of their bed mumbling something about having to get up so early.

"I'll meet you in the café in about ten minutes," he instructed. "I'm going to wake up the girls and then take a look at the car."

Their father departed the room and the boys laid back down on the bed to squeeze in a few more minutes of rest. Jake stuck his head back into the room, "anyone not in the café in ten minutes goes without breakfast," he announced.

He shut the door quickly, not giving them a chance to respond. Both boys feet hit the floor at the same time.

"Boy, what a slave driver," Josh complained as he rounded up his clothes.

"Yea, what's the hurry?" agreed Little Jake.

Josh finished dressing first and made his way to the door.

"I'll wait for you outside slowpoke. By the way, little brother, you've got your shorts on backward."

Josh was out the door fast as Little Jake's tennis shoe came flying at him.

Jake had finished eating first and made his way to the parking lot to check the car before moving on. He was a little concerned about the cooling system as the car seemed to heat up going over the passes in Utah. For the most part it had been a nice journey and everyone seemed happy and excited about the trip. He had the hood up on the car and was inspecting the radiator as Maggie and the kids came out of the café and joined him. Finding no indication of trouble, he closed the hood and cleaned his hands on a rag. Maggie was in awe of the mountains.

"Have you ever seen anything so beautiful?" she asked.

"I know this Maggie, it's sure not Kansas", came Jake's reply.

"Is California this beautiful Jake?" she inquired.

"I don't know Maggie. Why don't we load up and go find out for ourselves", came his reply.

Little Jake made a dash for the front seat, exclaiming it was his turn to sit up front.

"Hey," Jake scolded, "where are your manners, young man? The lady sits up front."

The boy would argue the point. "Oh come on Pa, she sat in front last time so it's my turn now!"

"It's alright Jake," said Maggie, "I'll sit in back with Beth."

Little Jake gave out a holler as he bounded into the front seat next to his Pa.

Jake started the car as he reached over and rustled his son's hair.

"You've sure got a way with the women, young man", said Jake as he headed the car down the road.

This time they were headed in a southerly direction.

As they made their way through Salt Lake City, toward Provo, Utah. Maggie mentioned to Jake that she had an aunt living there and maybe she might be better off to go there and stay with her for awhile. Although she hadn't seen her for many years, it would give her time to think about her future and to mend her wounds.

Not really anxious to stop, Jake reminded her of the bruises on her face and suggested she call her the next time they gassed up, knowing full well they would be well beyond Salt Lake. She agreed to do it another time and leaned back in her seat for the rest of the day's journey. One thing that really bothered her was not knowing where she fit into Jake's plan or if she really was a part of his plan. For the moment, however, she felt safe and thus dedicated herself to watching the beautiful Utah scenery.

Traveling due South from Salt Lake, the highway paralleled the Wasatch mountain range with beautiful Mt. Timpanogas towering over Lake Utah to the West. They saw road signs along the way with unfamiliar names, such as American Fork, Provo and Spanish Fork.

Near Provo, they exited the North, South highway and headed southeast into the mountains. They made their way through beautiful little towns as canyons after canyons passed them by. There ware small streams cutting their way through the red and orange rocks that made up the landscape.

One by one, the passengers began to doze off while Jake was busy watching for rocks on the road. Finally, the road crested a small summit and Jake's sigh of relief was short lived as steam started pouring out from under the hood.

"Well damn," yelled Jake as he searched the road ahead for a place to pull off.

"What's the matter Jake?" Maggie asked as the car made a bumpy exit onto the shoulder of the road.

Beth grabbed Maggie's hand while Josh was being bounced around in the rear of the station wagon. Everyone began talking at once, so Jake raised his hands above his head as he brought the car to a halt.

25

"I'm sure everything is alright," he proclaimed, "I think we have a radiator problem so everyone calm down while I check it out."

Jake stepped out of the car and tried to stretch his legs a bit. Maggie rolled down her window and asked Jake if they could get out of the car and stretch as well. He said they could, but to sit over by the dirt bank, away from the road.

Maggie took Beth and Little Jake over to a big rock, next to a small stream, and sat down. Josh got the toolbox out of the car and sat it in front of the car where Jake was standing.

Jake asked Josh to get him the canteen and a towel from a box on the rack. Josh retrieved the items and handed them to Jake. After using the towel to take the radiator cap off, Jake inspected the hoses.

"Do you think we blew a hose Pa," inquired Josh.

"Hoses seem to be alright but there could be a leak in one somewhere", Jake answered.

Josh watched as Jake poured water into the radiator from the canteen.

"I don't see anything coming out of the hoses Pa", exclaimed Josh.

Jake stopped pouring the water into the radiator, sat the canteen on top of the radiator and stood leaning on the car with both hands. He looked down at his feet, which were soaking wet.

"Josh ", he said softly", I believe we have a busted radiator."

"How can you tell Pa?" asked Josh.

Jake reached over and took his son by the shoulder and bent him over so he could see Jakes shoes.

"Because I'm standing in a puddle of water," Jake replied.

Josh pulled away, turning and laughing and laughing some more as he made his way over to where Maggie and the kids were sitting.

"Not very funny Josh," said Maggie. "Now we're stuck."

Josh just couldn't contain himself as he was now bent over in laughter while holding his side.

"Can't help it Maggie. If you could have seen the look on Pa's face when the water filled his shoes. It was almost like he peed his pants."

Soon they were all laughing, except Jake, who saw no humor in it at all as he sat on the running board of the car to change into a dry pair of shoes. He stood up and began to motion with his arms for them to get back into the car.

"All you happy people can get back into the car now."

Jake took the empty canteen down to the stream and filled it again and then poured it into the radiator.

Everyone was asking the same question as they piled back into the car. How were they going to go anywhere with a busted radiator? Jake got behind the steering wheel and released the hand brake.

"Saw a sign a few miles back about a town called Thistle. Shouldn't be too far down the road and there should be a gas station there. I'm going to try and coast it in, so hang on and be quiet until we get there," Jake ordered.

They had been coasting for about a mile when some buildings appeared on the right side of the road. The road gave way to a huge parking lot that fronted a café and a 'Flying A" gas station. Jake turned the car off the pavement and onto the dirt leading to the garage and gas pumps. In a cloud of dust, Jake eased the car next to one of the pumps and stopped. Maggie had forgotten to roll up her window and dust was everywhere. They were all coughing as they got out of the car.

"Oh my God. Have you ever seen so much dust?" Maggie complained.

Jake answered, "Yep, I have. Last year in Kansas and it couldn't have happened to a nicer group of passengers."

As they stood there, letting the dust settle, they had their first glimpse of their newly found stop over.

"Look," said Jake, "why don't all of you go into the café and have some lunch and I'll join you after I take care of business here."

They all turned and began making their way toward the café.

"Kind of dusty around here Maggie," Little Jake observed as tiny currents of air swirled the dirt before them.

"Yea, and look how dingy the café looks. We're liable to get food poisoning in here," Josh chimed in.

"Now, now, it's not as though we have to live here. We'll be on our way as soon as the car is fixed," Maggie cautioned.

They entered the café and selected a table by a large front window. Josh was looking out the window at the two men looking at the car. Once again Josh began to laugh uncontrollably.

"What's so funny Josh?"

"I can't help it Maggie. If you could have seen the look on Pa's face when that water soaked his shoes," Josh explained.

Maggie handed Josh a menu and told him he'd better put a lid on the laughter before Jake came in and gave him something to smile about. They all giggled as they got down to the business of ordering their lunches.

Jake had propped his foot on the bumper of the car, watching the old man inspect the radiator.

"Well, how bad is it?"

"A little patience, my man," came the reply.

"I want to make sure my diagnosis is correct before I give you the bad news."

"Well how bad is it?"

"I'm afraid your radiator is split open at the seam," he replied.

"Can you fix it?"

"Nope," the man answered as he wiped his hands on an old oily rag.

"The gap is too wide and besides, I don't own a welding machine any more."

"So, what do we do now?"

"That's up to you, young feller," came the reply. "If you can afford a new one, I'll send the boy into Price to pick it up."

Jake pulled out a cigar from his shirt pocket and stuffed it into his mouth as he pondered the situation.

"How long will that take?"

"Not long at all if you light that cigar," came the reply as the old man pointed to the 'No Smoking' sign between the pumps.

"Oh, sorry," said Jake as he put the cigar back into his pocket.

The old man smiled as he thought of an answer to the question.

"Maybe one, two days at the most. Depends on if they have a radiator this size in stock."

"How come so long?"

"There's a war on you know, hard to stock up on car parts. Now if you were driving a tank..."

"Never mind. I get the picture," conceded Jake.

"Well, come on into the office and I'll call the parts store in Price to see if they can help," urged the old man.

The owner went into the office as Jake opened the lid to the soft drink cooler and reached into the ice water to fetch a 'Nesbit Orange' soda. He opened it on the opener on the side of the cooler. As he reached the door, he couldn't help but notice a small flag with a gold star in the middle of it, displayed in the window. What caught his eye even more was the "For Sale by Owner" sign hanging next to it.

The old man was on the phone to the parts store as Jake entered the office and sat down. Turns out they had a radiator to fit the car and arrangements were made to pick it up that afternoon.

"Couldn't help noticing the Gold Star in the window. Someone in your family die in the war?"

The old man sat in silence as he filled his pipe with tobacco and lit it. Jake sat in silence also, giving the man time to gather his thoughts. As the smoke rose from the pipe, the man told his story.

"It was our Grandson, Lenny. He is our daughter's boy from Arizona. He and most of the boys from his graduating class couldn't wait to enlist and get into the fight. He joined the Air Force and became a pilot and was stationed in England. He was on a mission over Germany where his plane was shot down.

"I'm sorry" said Jake. "I shouldn't have asked."

"No, no that's alright. I find it helps to talk about it now and then."

"Why did you pick this place to move to," Jake asked.

"Well, about five years ago, after Lenny graduated from high school, the misses and I decided we'd had enough of Los Angeles' big city living, so we packed it all up and went looking for a quiet place to live. We fell in love with Thistle with its little stream and the quiet of the evenings. It took all our savings, but for us, it was worth it. Funny though, now that Lenny's gone, it just doesn't seem important any more."

"What are your plans if you sell out?" inquired Jake.

"Oh, simple enough, I guess. Take the money and head for Arizona. We have a small piece of land there."

Jake took a piece of paper from his wallet, unfolded it and handed it to the old man.

"Is the asking price in your ad still the same?" asked Jake.

"Well," said the old man. "I guess it does pay to advertise after all.

Which paper did you find this in?"

"The 'Farm and Ranch Monthly', a couple of weeks ago," came the reply.

The old man tossed it back on the desk.

"Nothing has changed, young man. That's my asking price and it's pretty firm."

Jake stood up and extended his hand across the table.

"I'm Jake Ritter from Kansas. The three children are mine and the young lady is a good friend of the family."

"I'm Jason Jarvis and my wife is Mattie," he replied. "You're welcome to stay in the cabins until your car is fixed. Why don't you join your family and have something to eat while I get to moving on this repair."

"If you don't mind Mr. Jarvis, I'm going to have a look around before we talk business."

As he reached the door, he turned and asked Jarvis not to mention anything about buying the place to the others. He wanted it to be a surprise. Having said that, he closed the door behind him and pulled out that cigar and lit it.

He walked to the front of the garage and looked in. It appeared to have all the necessary equipment for a good operation. He puffed on the cigar as he walked passed the front of the café. The kids were waving their arms at him to come in and join them for lunch.

"I'll be there in a few minutes," he yelled back.

They acknowledged what he had said and returned to their meal. Jake continued on up the path, which led to the five cabins. They were located at the base of a small hill, about ten feet apart from one another.

This is perfect, he thought. Josh and he could operate the garage and gas station. With all the experience he had on the farm, fixing the tractors and equipment, he was confident he would be able to handle the repairs on cars and trucks.

Maggie could run the café, with a little help, while Beth and Little Jake could take care of the cabins, cleaning up and changing the linens. Of course, when he wasn't busy in the garage, he would be available to help out wherever needed.

The excitement of it all was growing inside of him as he made his way toward a small cluster of buildings by the railroad tracks. The door was open at one of the smaller buildings and Jake noticed two men sitting at a table playing cards. The older of the two men spoke as Jake entered the room.

"Good afternoon. What can I do for you?"

"Good afternoon. Just taking a look around. Do all the trains stop here?"

"Not all trains. The troop trains stop here to take on water and to let the troops take a break. Old man Jarvis sets tables out and serves coffee and doughnuts to the boys."

"How often do they come through," inquired Jake.

"Oh, once or twice a week, maybe more. The regular passenger trains use the spur track when the freight trains come through but the passengers aren't allowed off the train," came the reply.

"I didn't know passenger trains gave way to freight trains," replied Jake.

"They do these days mister. With the war on and everything, those freights have the right of way. They carry the materials needed for all those war plants in California."

Jake walked over to the table and asked if he could join them for a minute. Having been invited to sit down, he pulled up another chair and joined them.

"I'm asking these questions because I may be interested in buying this place and I'm trying to get some idea of the operation.

"You looking to buy this place from old man Jarvis?"

Jake took a puff off of his cigar and flicked the ashes into the ashtray on the table.

"Could be, if the price is right and the set up can be a money maker for me and the family."

"Well I'll say this for the old man, he wants out of here in the worst way. The way he and the misses feel right now, a guy could bargain for a good price. They lost their Grandson in the war, you know?"

"So I hear," Jake said as he stood up. "Well thank you for your time and information, you've been a great help."

Jake exited the building and stood outside and faced the café, giving him a perfect view of the property. He imagined there were about five acres or so of usable land. Beyond the fence line, at the rear of the property, were rolling hills and a few sagebrush.

He straightened his hat and made his way toward the café, all the time puffing on that cigar, knowing full well he had found the perfect set-up that fit his dreams of independence. He wasn't fooling himself; however, as he realized that buying it was one thing, asking Maggie and the kids to give up the idea of California, was another. As he entered the café, he reminded himself that no one could keep him from his dream.

Chapter Four

Sheriff Manson was busy at his desk as a stranger entered his office. The man was well dressed and carried a brief case.

"How may I help you this morning?" asked the Sheriff.

"I'm looking for Sheriff Boone Manson. Might that be you?"

"I'm Sheriff Manson", came the reply. "What can I do for you today?"

He motioned for the man to sit down at the desk as he himself sat back down on the other side.

"I'm trying to locate the Ritter farm and Jake Ritter but I've been told he and his family no longer live there."

Manson didn't answer right away. He took a cigarette from his pack and lit it.

"And who might you be, if you don't mind my asking?"

"Oh, I'm sorry," came the reply. "My name is Gerald Clauson and I represent Kansas State Farm Insurance out of Kansas City. I'm an insurance investigator."

"Well you're right Mr. Clausen, the Ritters moved out three days ago headed for California. Is there anything I can do for you?"

"Not really, I guess. I was hoping to talk with Mr. Ritter concerning the fire at his farm that destroyed his house and killed his wife."

"Well, I'm afraid you're a little late for that. Like I said before, Jake took the insurance money, along with the money from the sale of his farm, and headed west."

Mr. Clausen opened his briefcase and withdrew a letter his company received through the mail.

"This is a letter our office received and I'm following up on it as it has some very strong allegations. He handed it over the desk to the sheriff who took it and read it out loud.

To Whom It May Concern:

I have reason to believe the Jake Ritter farm fire was set by Jake himself and should be investigated."

Signed, Melvin Trask

"That's old man Trask who lives on the hill with his wife and three girls, but I don't know how much credence you can put into anything he says."

"Why is that sheriff?"

"Trask and his wife are hard drinkers and rule over the girls with a firm hand, with hand being the operative word. From what I've been told by my sources, the old man got into a huge fight with his oldest daughter, Maggie, the night before the Ritters left for California. The next morning the fight escalated and reached the point where Maggie pulled a knife on her dad just as the Ritters drove up to say good-bye to her. Fearing for her life, she ran out the back door of the house, with her father chasing her with a shotgun, and got into the front seat of the Ritter automobile. The car sped away in a hail of buckshot from the old man's back porch."

Having said that, the sheriff slid the letter back across the desk to Clausin who picked it up and placed it back into the briefcase.

"Well sheriff, I think I'll go up to the Trask place and have a chat with the old man and then take in your fair city, if you don't mind?"

The sheriff stood up and walked Clausin to the door and opened it for him.

"Feel free to make yourself at home and I'll be around if you need anything further. Sorry I don't know where the Ritters are in

California."

Clausin shook the sheriff's hand and exited the office. The sheriff watched as the man looked up and down the street and finally got into his car and drove away.

Ж

The family had been given the bad news by Mr. Jarvis that it would take two days to fix the car. With no options open to them for continuing the trip, Jake rented two cabins, one for him and the boys and one for the girls.

Actually, Jake looked on the delay as a blessing, for it gave him ample time to sort out, in his mind, the approach he would use to sell the idea of buying Thistle to his family. He had been noticeably deep in thought throughout the afternoon and into the evening.

It was near bedtime now and Jake knew if he were to put his plan into motion he would have to present it to Maggie and the children immediately. The cabins had complete cooking facilities so Maggie had baked a cake and Beth made some hot chocolate so they could have a snack before they turned in.

The girls were busy preparing the food as Jake and the boys took their places around the table. Jake nervously tapped the table top with his fingers as he waited. There was a silence about the room as Maggie and the children eyed one another, looking for confirmation that each was aware that Jake had something on his mind. Josh broke the silence.

"So Pa, how much further to California?"

"Oh I don't know Josh. It depends on how much time we spend seeing the countryside between here and there."

"Hey Pa," Little Jake chimed in, "is it true the sun shines all the time in California and you can swim in the ocean?"

"I reckon that's what people say alright but there ain't no place that's perfect. I'm sure even California gets its share of rain and fog."

Maggie brought the cake to the table and sat it in front of Jake. She looked at the children as she placed her hand on Jake's shoulder.

"Come on Jake, what's on your mind?"

"What do you mean by that Maggie?" Jake snapped back. He was upset with himself for letting all of them read him so easily.

"Come on Pa", chimed in Josh. "You've been quiet ever since we got here and that's not like you."

Jake sat silent looking down at the cake sitting before him, making sure he made no eye contact with any of them. He was feeling guilty about California and for a second he felt trapped. Beth and Maggie joined the boys at the table. No one could imagine what could possibly be wrong, other than the car being broken. They sat quietly eating, looking up at Jake every so often, expecting him to say something.

"Might as well tell us Pa" said Little Jake. "We're all in this together."

Jake continued to eat his cake without answering or looking up. Beth placed her hand on Jake's arm as if to assure him it would be alright. He looked around the table at each of them and realized there was no way out now, for each of them was eager to hear what he had to say. He took another bite of cake and then pushed the cake away. They watched as he pulled a cigar from his pocket and they realized whatever was on Jake's mind would be forthcoming.

Maggie was upset when she saw the cigar.

"Must you smoke that cigar in here? Can't you just tell us what the matter is?"

"Let him smoke" suggested Little Jake, "he does his best thinking when he's chewing on one of them."

Josh looked over at his little brother.

"Boy, for a little guy, you sure have a lot to say."

"Well I'm part of this family too, even if I am the youngest."

Jake, seeing an argument about to ensue because of his silence, broke into the conversation.

"Alright, alright. I'll tell you what's on my mind. Just all of you calm down."

Jake got up and began circling the table, cigar in mouth but unlit, trying to find the right words to say. All eyes were upon him as silence prevailed. Realizing there were no 'right' words to say, he decided to just lay it all on the table and tell it like it was. He made his way around the table and stood behind an empty chair where he placed both hands on the top of the backrest.

"Here it is in a nutshell. This place is up for sale and I think we ought to buy it."

All eyes were upon him and they bore down on him like a runaway freight train. The only thing he could do was to keep talking.

"Now I know what you're thinking and I can understand you're being upset, but let's all be calm about this and at least talk it out."

Josh objected immediately.

"But you said we were going to California to start a new life and that's why we all voted to leave Kansas."

"Yea, what about the sunshine and swimming in the ocean?" chimed in Little Jake.

Beth sat quietly with her hands folded in her lap, staring at her plate. Maggie had her arm around Beth's shoulder as she looked at Jake.

"The boys are right Jake," she said in a soft voice, not wanting to get into a shouting match. "You promised all of us California."

"I know I did and at the time it was a great idea but here's a chance for all of us to make a great living."

Caught up in the excitement of his own idea, he began to circle the table while gesturing with his hands and arms as he spoke. It was like he was in some sort of trance. Then came his explanation.

"I see it this way. If we go on to California, what's going to happen? I'll end up working in one of those plane factories with who knows what kind of hours. Maggie, you'll have to get a job somewhere and right now the only work you know is waitress work. You'll be working for someone else for a few bucks an hour and tips.

You and I will be working, so I'll have to hire someone to watch Little Jake until either Josh or Beth gets home. Who knows, Josh and Beth will probably end up in a large school, one where kids seem to get lost in the shuffle."

Maggie stood up and carried away a few plates to the drain board. Josh was the first to speak.

"How does our staying here change anything? You and Maggie will still have to work and Beth and I will still have to go to school, wherever that will be," he said with a sarcastic tone in his voice.

"Don't you see? We would own all of this and all of us would share in the running of it. Josh, you and I could run the gas pumps and I could do the mechanic work and when you're in school I could handle it myself. Beth and Little Jake could take care of the cabins. You know, keep them clean and change the linens.

Jake turned and faced Maggie, who stood facing the sink, listening.

"Maggie, you could run the café and be your own boss."

She turned and faced Jake and with a half grin on her face she answered him.

"What makes you think being a waitress for you is any easier than for someone in California? I wanted to go to California to make a new start for myself, maybe learn a new trade so I wouldn't have to sling hash anymore."

Before Jake could answer, Josh had his say also.

"Besides Pa, I want to go to a high school with a good baseball program. I'll probably end up at some rinkey dink school that never heard of the game."

Jake put his cigar into his mouth and stood with his hands on his hips and mumbled something about people not listening to him and bullheadedness. He turned back to Maggie, as if asking for support for his plan.

"What do you say Maggie?"

She looked at the children and then back at Jake and answered.

"I say it's late and we should all get some rest. I think this calls for a family discussion and I'm not part of the family."

Jake walked over to Maggie and placed his hands on her shoulders and, with a smile on his face, confronted her.

"Of course you're a part of this family. We're all in this together and by sticking together we can do anything."

"No I don't know that and I don't know that I even want to be part of any family."

She stepped away from Jake and walked toward the door.

"Don't go now", he pleaded, "We haven't made a decision yet."

Maggie opened the door and then turned to face Jake once again. It was evident she was very unhappy and upset.

"Look Jake", she said. "what you and the children decide to do is your business because you are a family. Deciding what is best for me will take some thought, so I'll give you my answer in the morning."

She left the room before Jake could say anything else and went to her cabin.

"Damn", he said as he slammed the cigar into the ashtray.

"What do you expect Pa", said Josh. "We all had our sights set on California. Now you try and sell us on this God forsaken place and you think we should feel good about it?"

Jake stared at his son until Josh had to finally look away, knowing full well he was witnessing an anger he had never seen before in his father. As quickly as it came, it went away.

Jake stood up once again and, with much resolve, pleaded with his children again.

"I didn't expect you to be thrilled with the idea but I do expect all of you to give our situation some serious thought. Really kids, it will all come down to this. I've got the responsibility of raising you and to do that I have to be able to make a good living so that you'll have clothes to wear, food to eat and a good home to live in.

I can understand your concerns about living in the dessert, schools and everything else that may be wrong in your eyes but you also have to consider my position. At least living here we would all live and work together as a family. Somewhere on your list of good and bad, you're going to be truthful about what will be best for all of us. I'm telling you now, I can meet the needs of this family better by staying here and making this a profitable business."

Jake took Beth's hand in his.

"I'm only asking all of you to think on it and give me your answer in the morning."

"Are we going to vote on it?" asked Little Jake.

"Ya, we've always taken a vote on important matters", said Josh.

"In the morning I'll listen to what all of you have to say and then I'll make the decision based on your input. There will be no vote this time because the final decision will be mine. There's too much at stake here."

Jake led Beth towards the door.

"Come on honey, I'll walk you to your cabin and you boys get into bed. I'll be right back."

"What about Maggie Pa? Is she going to go away?"

"I don't know kids. She'll have to make up her own mind and hopefully she'll decide to stay on with us."

When Jake and Beth reached the cabin, they saw Maggie sitting on the front porch stairs. She was making designs in the dirt with a small branch from a tree. Jake kissed Beth on the cheek and said goodnight.

"I'll be in shortly sweetie," said Maggie, "I want to talk with your father for a moment."

Beth entered the cabin and Jake sat on the stairs beside Maggie. He looked around at the moonlit desert under a cloudless sky. The outcroppings stood out like silent guardians for as far as the eye could see.

"Kind of beautiful, in their own way, don't you think?"

"I guess so, under the right conditions, but I'll bet it can get pretty nasty in the winter."

"Well I guess there's good and bad no matter where you live. I know it may be a little soon to ask but have you given any thought to my proposition?"

"You know Jake," she began, "you really surprised all of us in there tonight and..."

Jake interrupted. "I know...."

Maggie wouldn't let Jake continue. She was really upset with Jake's handling of the situation and he could tell by the sound of her voice she was very angry.

"No Jake, let me finish first. You had us all pumped up about going to California when we left Wheaton. You painted a rosy little picture for all of us and we accepted that because none of us had too much going for us at the time. Speaking for myself, I guess I'm grateful to you for giving me a way out of a hopeless situation, however, I am twenty-one years old and somewhere down the line I want to meet someone, fall in love, settle down and raise a family together."

"I want that for you too Maggie if that's what you want. All I'm saying is we all have a better chance of being together and working together if we stay here. Sure, it's an out-of-the-way road stop and yes, it's located on the edge of the desert, but that's the beauty of it Maggie. It'll all be ours and I know that we can make a go of it."

"No Jake, it'll all be yours because it's what you want to do with your life and that's fine for you. Have you given any thought about the kids and me? We have our dreams too you know."

Jake got to his feet and began pacing back and forth. Maggie knew she had touched on a sore spot when she mentioned baseball. Jake spun around and faced Maggie as he spoke.

"Baseball... baseball... that's all I hear out of him these days."

"Well, what's wrong with baseball for heavens sakes? Josh happens to be very good at it and everyone says so, except you."

Jake was riled up now and took advantage of the opportunity to vent his thoughts on the subject.

"There's nothing wrong with playing baseball Maggie, it just happens to be like all other professional sports. It's every kid's dream to be like Babe Ruth or Stan Musial; but for the few that make it in the big time there are thousands of youngsters who will not have the talent to be a professional ball player. If that's their only dream and they fail then what do they have to fall back on? I want to give Josh something solid and proven as a foundation. A craft he can build on and make a living at."

There was a long silence as Maggie considered what Jake had just told her. She stood up and put her arm around the porch beam and looked toward the lighted café. As she spoke, her eyes welled up with tears.

"You know Jake, up until this moment I never questioned leaving my family and running off with you and the kids this way. I guess I looked at it through the eyes of a child, like riding a rollercoaster for the first time. It's a thrilling experience doing it and then, all of a sudden, the ride has ended and reality sets in. I don't know if running away has solved my problems. I think I took the easy way out."

"You took the only way out your father left open to you Maggie," Jake said.

"That may be true Jake and maybe by leaving I spared myself a few more beatings but I'm finding out it hurts worse not knowing how my sisters are doing. It hurts inside because I ran away and my being here means I can't help them now."

Jake walked over to her and placed his hands on her shoulders as she looked down crying. He reached down and put a hand under her chin and forced her face upward.

"Look at me Maggie," he pleaded. "Sure you're going to question yourself about leaving but it's a two way street. If you had stayed you would always have wondered if it might have been better if you had left. I think it's better this way Maggie. At least you have a chance to make something of your life and I'm not saying you have to stay here the rest of your life. All I am saying is at least by helping me run this place you can make a start for yourself. You'll be able to put some money away and then, when "Mr. Right" comes along, you'll be in a better position to pick up and start a new life."

Maggie turned and scanned the horizon.

"Do you honestly believe someone for me will come through this God-forsaken canyon some day?"

"I can't answer that for you Maggie, but I'll promise you this. When the day comes you want to leave, for whatever reason, I'll back you one hundred percent."

She looked him straight in the eyes.

"You can honestly promise me that Jake?"

Jake took one step back and raised his right hand.

"You have my word on it, so help me God."

Maggie turned and walked toward the door and as she opened it she spoke to Jake.

"I'll let you know in the morning how I feel about it all. Good night Jake."

Meanwhile, Josh and Little Jake had gotten into bed, both lying there on their backs with their hands behind their heads, staring at the ceiling as the café lights streamed across the room.

"What are you thinking about Josh?"

"You know what I'm thinking about little brother."

"Ya, I guess so Josh. What are you going to tell Pa in the morning?"

"I don't know. I'm thinking on it."

"I'm thinking on it too," replied Little Jake.

It felt good to him that Josh had included him in this important decision making conversation. It made him feel needed and a part of something so important to the family. After a short silence he spoke again.

41

"Josh, even when we make up our minds, how will we know we chose right?"

"That's the hard part, little brother, because you never know what lies ahead, no matter which road you choose to take. You just have to sort things out, make a decision and then hope for the best."

"Is Pa hoping for the best Josh?"

"I suppose so. I guess he feels the best way to care for us is to buy this place and make a go of it."

"Is that the best for us Josh?"

"I don't know. Pa thinks so. I don't think Pa is asking us whether we want to stay here or not. I think he's asking us to put our trust in him, a kind of vote of confidence as our father."

Little Jake turned over on his side and pulled the covers up over his head.

"It sure gets complicated Josh."

"Go to sleep little brother. You'll have the answers in the morning, just like the rest of us."

As was his custom, Jake was up and dressed at first light. He found it hard to break the habits, so necessary and regimented, that came from operating a farm in Kansas. All the requirements for a successful farmer had been instilled in him by his father from as far back as he could remember. He was thankful now for what his father had taught him to do.

He was no stranger to hard work or hard times for that matter. Jake had shared, with his father, the bitter cold of many winters, the overwhelming heat of unforgiving summers. Jake realized early on his father's tenacious ways were his way of showing Jake how to survive under any conditions. Jake always admired his father's steadfastness and unrelenting stands on the decisions which always confronted him.

Jake knew also that on this very day he would have to reach back and muster for himself his father's convincing attitude that no matter what lay ahead, his decision would be the right one. Convincing the others of that was the real challenge. It was the trump card only he could hold when he dealt the final hand.

He placed upon the table three envelopes, three sheets of paper and three pencils. He used a cup to prop up the note he had written and left in the middle of the table. He put on his coat and quietly went outside and made his way toward the beckoning lights of the café.

The note was as follows……..

Good morning..

"As you all know, this morning you are to vote on staying here and buying this place and making a home and life for all of us. If the vote is to stay then each of us will be responsible for helping with the chores and actual work. In return, you will be paid a decent wage for time worked.

I want each of you to write down what is most important to you if we stay here and if at all possible I will see to it your needs are met. I will have the final say in this matter.

However, I will consider all input from you."

Love…Dad

P.S. Josh, help your brother with his writing.

Jake sat in a booth by the window, sipping his coffee and watching the beauty that is the desert unfolding in the light of dawn. He couldn't tell if it was the beauty of the vast scene before him or the quiet serenity of it that gave him that feeling of comfort and belonging. Whatever it was, he knew it was something special to him, something he felt must be a part of his life. His deep thoughts were interrupted by Maggie's voice.

"Good morning Jake. May I join you?"

Startled, Jake stood up and motioned to the empty side of the booth.

"Of course Maggie, please sit down. Would you like some breakfast? Oh miss, could we have a menu please?"

The waitress picked up a menu and a fresh pot of coffee and made her way to their table. Maggie turned her cup right side up but said she'd eat later.

Nothing was said as she added a little cream and sugar to her coffee. She didn't bother to look up as she stirred her coffee ever so slowly. She was aware of Jake's anxiety, like a little boy waiting for someone to tell him he could keep the puppy that had followed him home.

"Did you sleep well Maggie?"

"Not really. You didn't expect any of us to sleep after the bomb shell you dropped on us last night?"

"I guess not but I don't have a lot of time to make Jarvis an offer on this place."

"Are you really sure this is what you want Jake? You haven't even asked to see the books to see if this is a money making proposition."

"Yes, this is what I want Maggie. I want it for me and the kids and you. It's a chance for all of us to work and stay together, a chance to have some control of our destiny. We'll be able to make our own decisions and not be at the mercy of someone who can fire you at the drop of a hat. Then what do you have? Now you're out pounding the pavement looking for work wondering where your next paycheck will come from. I may sound a little upset with the question and maybe I am but by God at least by staying here I can acquire what is needed to raise my kids and see to it I give them some kind of foundation for the future."

He leaned back in the booth and contemplated her question about checking the books and making sure a living could be made there. He knew it was a legitimate question and needed to be answered.

"Maggie, it doesn't make any difference to me if Jarvis is making a go of it here. With what plans I have for Thistle we can't help but make a good living here."

She had sat quietly while listening to Jake, trying to make sense of it all. Finally, she took a sip of coffee and smiled at him.

"Jake, I have been listening to you explain this dream of yours and I believe I understand what you're saying and I've given your proposition a lot of thought."

Jake leaned toward the table and reached across it and took Maggie's hand.

"Then you've made up your mind and you're going to stay?"

"Yes, I've made up my mind."

"That's really great Maggie and I know you'll never regret it."

"No Jake. I've made up my mind to move on and take my chances in California."

44

Jake released her hand and flung himself back against the booth. He knew that being upset with her wasn't the answer to his problem. Somehow he had to convince her to stay. He decided on the negative approach.

"My God Maggie, you can't go on to California alone. You don't even have the money to get there, let alone survive until you get your first check."

She looked at him in disbelief, not wanting to believe what he had just said. It certainly wasn't the response she had hoped for.

"I was hoping you could lend me enough to hold me over until I got my first paycheck and a place to live. I'll pay you back when I get to working."

Jake was really stunned at what he was hearing. He couldn't believe this girl, who had never in her life been out of Wheaton , Kansas, would even consider taking on such a challenge.

"I can't believe you've made this decision when you haven't even heard my proposition Maggie."

"What proposition Jake? To be a waitress in this dinky café, working for tips for God knows how long. Do you call that a future? The only thing different by staying here and living in Wheaton is the beatings."

"Well Hell Maggie, at least that's a start."

She leaned forward and looked Jake straight in the eyes because she wanted him to understand what she was about to say.

"Look Jake, anywhere I go will be a start for me. I told you before, I don't want to be a waitress all my life. I want to get married and settle down and have children of my own."

"But that time will come Maggie, I promise you."

"Will it Jake? Do you honestly believe anyone of substance will come through that door that I would really be interested in? This isn't even a city or town. This is a hole-in-the-wall garage and greasy spoon café with a few cabins thrown in for good measure."

Jake was getting very irritated with her at this point. He felt as though she wasn't paying attention to what he was saying. He was quick to defend his choice for his investment.

"See there Maggie, you haven't even been listening to what I've been telling you. I'm not going to invest in this place and let it fall

45

down around us. I've got plans and ideas to redo the entire layout. The cabins will be redone inside with new furniture and fixtures. I'm going to expand this main dinning area to double the seating capacity. There'll be a long counter just in front of the kitchen and the storage room will be double the size it is now."

Maggie noticed that his eyes seemed to gleam as he spoke, especially when he came to the part about fixing up the garage.

"I'm going to install those new gas pumps and build a canopy over them. The garage will be doubled in size and will house every tool and machine available to make it a class 'A' repair shop. Hell Maggie, the war is going our way now and soon it will be over. When the rationing ends people will be traveling again and I intend to give those travelers a comfortable and reliable place for all their needs." Maggie listened with great interest as he placed before her his entire dream. Here was a man who was setting a course for himself and was determined to follow it through to the end.

"You're really going to go through with all this, aren't you Jake?"

"You bet your life I'm going to do it Maggie and I want you and the kids to be a part of it."

She leaned back and mulled over all that had been said. Was it all just a pipe dream? Was it wise to make his dream your dream too?

"You sure paint a good picture Jake Ritter. Just how would I fit into it all?"

Jake knew at that moment he held her interest enough to convince her to stay on. He knew also he'd have to come up with a substantial offer to make it worth her while. Without her knowledge of the restaurant business and her interest in his children and their well being he would be at a disadvantage. He felt Maggie was well worth the investment.

"How about this Maggie, I can't possibly operate the garage and oversee the café and cabins. Besides, I don't know doodly squat about running a café. But you do and so I want you to be in charge of its operation. How's that?"

"That won't work Jake. It's a full time job just being a waitress, let alone managing a busy café. With all the ordering and bookwork there's not a person alive that could handle that load for very long."

Jake thought about what she had said and realized she was right.

If he set it up the way he wanted it would definitely need a full time person to make it go.

Maggie sat there silently waiting for his response, knowing full well she had just put him into a situation he hadn't bargained for. She also realized that this was the time to make a move for herself and her future. Finally Jake spoke.

"You're right Maggie, it is too much of an operation for one person under those conditions, so how about this. We hire enough waitresses to cover all shifts and you do what's necessary to keep the place running and I'll pay you a monthly salary."

Now Maggie was getting excited for she realized a plan that would enable her to make a future for herself that included getting her sisters out from under her parents' domination. She knew it was a long shot but she had to take it... now.

"I've got a better solution Jake and you probably won't like it but I'm going to put it on the table because I have my dreams and future to think of also."

"Alright, go ahead, I'm listening."

This was it for her and she realized the importance of how she presented it to Jake. She chose her words very carefully.

"You want to buy Thistle and that's fine with me. From what you've told me this morning I can understand your interest in it. What you have to understand is my situation and what my goals are. So, knowing my concern for my sisters' well being and what I expect to achieve in my lifetime I make you this offer: once you've made all the improvements on this place, I want you to lease the café to me with a monthly payment set at an amount that will repay you for your investment. Secondly, you will completely stock the café with whatever it takes to get it going for the first few months since I don't have any money. Once the place is making money, I will be responsible for its entire operation, which will include any repairs or fixtures needed."

"Hold on there just a minute Maggie. Don't you think that's asking a little too much from someone who doesn't even have to put up a dime in the project?"

"Not at all Jake. You need someone to run this café and if not me, then who? Besides, I'll watch out for your children's well being. Now find someone out here that will do that for you."

Jake leaned back in the seat and pulled out a cigar and put it into his mouth. He toyed with it as he considered Maggie's offer. Finally, he looked her in the eyes and gave her his answer.

"You drive a hard bargain Maggie. Deep down in my heart I know you are right. If you leave here now I'd have a giant mess on my hands with the kids. I'd also have to hire someone to run this place and let's face it, you are good at both jobs."

The waitress made her way to their booth and informed Jake there was no pipe or cigar smoking allowed in the café.

"It's not even lit for God's sake," Jake replied.

"Makes no difference. Customers see that thing in your mouth and they won't even come inside."

Jake looked around the café in disbelief.

"There's no one in here but us."

She leaned down and spoke softly into his ear with a kind of finality in her voice.

"If you don't throw it away, I'll have to ask you to leave."

Maggie was giggling behind her menu for she knew how Jake felt about people telling him what to do. Jake returned the cigar to his shirt pocket.

"Tell you what mama, I'll put it away for now but I can guarantee you that at breakfast tomorrow I will smoke this cigar at this table."

"And I'll tell you what, mister arrogance, if you smoke that in here tomorrow I'll have you thrown out."

Ж

Beth was the first of the children to wake up and get dressed. Finding herself alone in the cabin she wondered where Maggie had gone. She made herself presentable and made her way to the other cabin where she knocked on the door. Not getting an answer, she entered the room and found Josh and Little Jake still asleep. She promptly shook Josh's bed until his head surfaced from beneath the covers.

"Awe come on Beth, give a guy a break," he complained as he rolled over and covered up his head once more.

Beth continued to shake the bed for she really enjoyed pestering Josh.

"For heaven's sake Beth, what's so important you have to wake us up at this hour?"

She handed Josh the note their father had left on the table for them. Josh grabbed the note and propped himself up on one elbow and began reading aloud. He lay back down on the bed and let out a big sigh.

"Come Little Jake, it's time to get up."

Maggie and Jake were just finishing eating as the three children exited the cabin and made their way toward the café.

"Well, here comes the bad news Maggie," Jake warned.

"Oh, I don't know that it will be bad news Jake. They followed you this far."

Jake fidgeted with his spoon as he watched the children and listened to what Maggie was telling him.

"Yes, but this isn't California either," Jake cautioned.

The good mornings were said as the kids took their places around the table. Not one of them gave any indication as to their feelings on the matter at hand.

"Boy, am I hungry," said Little Jake.

"Not so fast here kids," Jake interrupted. "Did you do what I asked you to do?"

Josh handed his father the three envelopes and sat down. He glanced over at Maggie but she just smiled and looked away.

Jake took the envelopes and motioned to the waitress to bring three glasses of orange juice for the kids. He waited until the juice was served and then went over the ground rules concerning the vote.

"As you know, majority rules as always and all will abide by the decision. I have made a special concession in this case because of the importance of this decision. Not only have I asked you for a vote, I've asked you for your opinions and suggestions. I will do everything in my power to make all of us happy no matter which way the vote goes. While I'm reading your comments you can go ahead and order your breakfast."

Jake sat the envelopes before him on the table as the waitress refilled his coffee cup. He glanced toward Maggie as he reached for the first envelope. For the first time since leaving Wheaton he felt very uneasy and unsure of what this outcome would be. The children ordered as he read the first letter in silence. It was from Beth.

Dear Pa,

"California sounded pretty good to all of us when you asked us to leave our home after mom died. It wasn't easy for us to leave our friends behind and to change schools and make new friends. I felt much like you did when mom died. You have always been a good father and you've always been there for us and taken good care of us. I put all my trust in you Pa, so if you feel our best chance at something good is to stay here in Thistle, then I vote to stay and make a go of it."

I Love You...Beth.

Jake folded the letter back up and placed it into the envelope. He looked around the table and without divulging who the writer was, simply told them it was one vote to stay.

The children looked at one another as Jake took a sip of coffee and opened the second envelope. The letter was from Josh.

Pa,

"As you know, I am upset with the idea of living here in this God forsaken place. I only have two years of high school left and you know my dream has always been to play baseball. I know you think baseball is just a game and there are more but I want baseball to be my life because I feel I'm good enough to play the game on a higher level. I feel if we stay here the school I will have to attend will not have a good athletic program whereas the California schools will. I feel you owe me a chance to be what I want to be."   Josh

Maggie watched Jake closely as he folded up the letter and put it back into the envelope. She detected a look of deep concern on his face. She looked away as he spoke.

"That's one vote for California."

The kids sat silently eating, just glancing at one another. None of them knew in what order the envelopes were being opened and they realized that, for the first time in their lives, they may be overruling the wishes of their father. Josh didn't know how Little Jake voted even though he wrote the letter for him. There were two boxes at the bottom of the paper; one marked 'stay' and one marked 'go'. Little Jake marked the one he wanted but neither Beth nor Josh knew which one he chose. Jake opened the last envelope and slowly unfolded it and silently read its contents.

Dear Pa,
    "I don't know how to vote because I don't know what California is or how it would be if we went. If we stay here and all be together then that's nice. California sounds fun too."
    Little Jake

P.S. "If we stay here then I want a bike and a dog."

    All eyes were on Jake now as he folded up the letter and returned it to the envelope. He leaned forward and folded his hands on the table as he spoke.
    "All the votes are counted and the majority say we stay here."
    Josh glared at his father as he got to his feet. He threw his napkin down on the table, pushed his chair back and stormed out of the café. Maggie reached for his arm as he went by but Josh just kept going.
    "Let him go Maggie. He needs some time to cool off," said Jake.
    Jake stood up and pulled some folded money from his wallet and dropped it on the table.
    "Would you mind sitting with the kids Maggie until they're finished eating? I'm going over and have a talk with Mr. Jarvis."
    "Sure Jake, you go on and we'll be just fine," she answered.
As Jake left the café he noticed Josh sitting on a nearby hill throwing rocks at a cactus. Good, Jake thought, he's getting rid of some of his hostility.
    The screen door slammed shut behind Jake as he entered the station office. The old man looked from the desk as Jake entered.
    "Makes a hell of a noise doesn't it?"
    "Gotta have it else the flies will pester you to death," replied the old man.
    He looked up again when Jake didn't answer.
    "Sent the boy for your part this morning. Should be back around

two."

Jake sat down in the empty chair next to the desk and pulled out a cigar from his pocket.

"Mind if I smoke?"

"No, no, go right ahead," answered the old man.

Jake lit his cigar and leaned back in his chair, settling in for some serious talking.

"What are you asking for the place Mr. Jarvis?"

"Why, you interested in buying Thistle?"

"Might be if the price is right and we can come to terms."

"Well, I own all of this free and clear so I can set the price whatever I want. There are no mortgages or loans outstanding and I paid cash for it so I expect to sell it for cash."

"You could be here a long time waiting for someone to come along with that kind of money Mr. Jarvis."

The old man got up and went over to the cola cooler across the room, lifted the lid and pulled out a Nesbitts Orange Crush from the icy water. He dried the bottle off with the towel hanging on the side of the case. He reached down and inserted the top of the bottle into the opener on the side of the case and popped the cap off. He took a long swig from the bottle as he patted his brow with his oily old rag from his overalls.

"Want one Mr.............

"Oh, I'm sorry. I'm Jake Ritter," he answered.

"Mr. Ritter?"

"No thanks, it's a little too early for me."

Jarvis returned to the desk and sat back down.

"Funny thing about buying and selling a place like this, young man. A young man like you, with a family to raise and all, looks at it as an investment in the future. Who knows, maybe even a dream come true. A place you can call your own where you can make an honest buck. A place away from the city life where you can keep an eye on your family."

"Well isn't that why you bought it in the first place?"

"That's true, but I don't dream anymore. My dreams died in the crash of a B-25 bomber that took my grandson's life. Funny thing, he told me freedom was worth fighting for and because of his efforts and others like him we will win this war. He fought for freedom and he is free now but I'll never be free because I'll always have to live with his memory. There is no freedom in knowing what was or the not knowing what might have been."

Jake, sensing the old man's sorrow, started to get up and leave. The old man put his hand on Jake's shoulder and quietly pushed him back into the seat.

"It's alright Mr. Ritter, I'm just an old man with a bitter taste in my mouth. I'm selling because there are too many memories for us here now and as each day passes it only gets worse."

"I'm sorry about your grandson Mr. Jarvis."

"Thank you, but enough of that. If you are interested in buying the place, and you have some cash, then let's talk particulars."

Jake was glad to hear Jarvis was ready to bargain and he felt a sense of excitement come over him.

"Well, I am interested and yes I do have some cash to invest if the price is right."

The old man went over to the open safe and withdrew a ledger and placed it in front of Jake.

"These are my books which show our daily input and expenses. Everything is in order but there is one thing you must remember. I don't advertise, pay rent and I buy most everything in bulk. As you can see, I don't have a lot of overhead. My wife runs the café and I run the garage. Our hired help consists of three people, the lady who helps in the café and a young boy who helps me run the station and garage."

"Who takes care of the cabins?"

"The cabins are more of a convenience than anything. When they are used the wife or I will go over and change the beds and clean up. With a little know how and ambition a man, like you, could make a gold mine out of this place."

Jake mulled over the ledger as he listened to the old man talk. He was disturbed by the running and laughing of Beth and Little Jake outside the building. Seeing them playing he realized there was one more important question he had to ask.

"What's the school situation here Mr. Jarvis?"

"Schools are in Price. The bus comes and picks them up in the morning and brings them home in the afternoon. There are always a few kids from the railroad shacks across the way that belong to the section crews."

"Do the schools have good sports programs?"

"The high school has about everything you'd want with an enrollment of about five hundred students. They are very competitive in athletics. They took the state championship in football when my grandson was a senior. He played halfback."

"What about baseball, do they have a good program?"

"Yes, a very good team since they hired Allen Cross as their coach. He really knows baseball alright."

"Is that the same Allen Cross that was involved in the Black Sox scandal a few fears back?"

"He was a rookie then and it was determined he had nothing to do with the 'fix' of the series."

Jake was relieved to hear that news. He hoped it would take away a lot of Josh's hostility about staying in Thistle.

"Well that sounds just great to me Mr. Jarvis," Jake said.

"In all fairness Mr. Ritter, there is something you should be aware of. If you think it's hot now you're mistaken. Summers here can get so hot you'd gladly crawl under a rock for a little shade. In the winter it can snow so hard and long that the trains can't even get through and the road closes. You just sit inside and drink coffee, waiting for the road crews to come and dig you out. However, the real danger is the rain."

"Why the rain?"

"Well, if you haven't noticed, Thistle is located on the banks of a creek that shifts ninety degrees in a southerly direction. It flows that way because of the solid rock formation on the west side."

"What are you saying, we could be flooded out?"

"It happened once in thirty-three; however, the water only covered the tracks and came up to the gas pumps. It rained for four straight days."

Jake closed the book and placed it back on the table.

"I think I've seen and heard enough to say I'm really interested in buying the place; so let's talk price."

"Well, if you're sure then here's my deal; but there are two concessions you have to agree to, no matter what the price."

Jake leaned back in the chair and puffed on his cigar once again wondering what kind of concessions Jarvis was talking about.

"What kind of concessions are you talking about Mr. Jarvis?"

"The first one involves the troop trains. They come through here quite often taking our boys to the ports in the West for shipment overseas. There is about an hour wait while the train is being serviced and it affords them a chance to get off the train and stretch a bit. When that happens, I've got tables set up down by the tracks at the depot where we serve donuts and coffee to those who want them and it's free."

Jake was relieved to hear such a minor request and answered quickly.

"I can agree to that. It's the least we can do for our fighting men in service."

"Yes and let's hope and pray this damn war is over before your children are old enough to join in."

"Amen to that," Jake chimed in.

"The second thing is a personal concern of mine but, if you want this place, you'll have to agree to the terms."

"And if I don't agree to a personal term, what happens?"

"If we can't come to terms on this I won't sell to you, plain and simple."

"Alright, what's the deal?"

"I don't know if you noticed the cook in the café or not. He's my third helper here."

"Yes I did. A colored fella, kind of quiet," acknowledged Jake.

"His name is Albert Washington. He was a member of a commando group making a 'behind the lines' raid on a German headquarters the day my grandson flew his mission over that same area. The plane was hit and went down in a field near Albert's command. Albert ran to the plane and pulled my grandson from the burning wreckage just as it exploded. The force of the blast broke both of Albert's ear drums while spraying gasoline scalded his hands and face. Without any regard for himself, he carried Wayne back to the safety of his command. He was awarded the Purple Heart for the wounds he received."

Jake listened as Jarvis relived that horrible event that took his grandson's life. How hard, he thought, for him to relive it all over again.

"What about your grandson?"

"Albert didn't know it at the time but Wayne was shot up and died before the plane crashed. He thought he saved Wayne's life and when he found out he hadn't, he cried. After he was released from the hospital and sent back home he came here just to tell us how sorry he was."

"And you offered him a job?"

"Yes. It turned out he was a cook in Chicago before the war. He had nowhere to go and was embarrassed about his disfigurement and scars. I promised him a job here for as long as he wanted it and it turns out that this is home to him now. It's really all he wants out of life. He makes me wonder sometimes, who is better off, Albert or my grandson."

"I'm really sorry for your loss Mr. Jarvis," said Jake.

Well the asking price is five thousand but if you'll agree to the terms of sale I'm willing to come down to four thousand."

The old man stood by the screen door watching the children playing. Jake got up and joined him at the door, still in awe at what was just said.

"You're willing to knock off a thousand just for coffee and donuts for the troops and for keeping on a cook? It doesn't make sense."

The old man had tears in his eyes as he answered in a whisper.

"Years ago I came here with a dream, much like you do today. I see your children playing and the excitement in your eyes at the prospect of having something of your very own and I am reminded of myself. For whatever reasons, Mr. Ritter, my offer stands at four thousand, take it or leave it."

"I'll take your offer, cash on the barrelhead."

The two men shook hands and returned to the desk.

"Done," said the old man. "I'll draw up the papers tonight. I'll have your car fixed by morning, and then you can go to the bank in Price and get a cashiers check."

"That's all there is to it?"

"You'll have to take the papers I give you to the court house so they can register the transaction and change the deed and title."

The two men shook hands once more as they made their way to the door. The old man opened the door for Jake.

"Go now Mr.Ritter and tell your family the good news."

Ж

As elated as Jake was, he still couldn't hide his concern for Josh's rebellion. He realized he had to come to grips with the situation immediately or things wouldn't run smoothly. He headed for the cabin he saw Josh enter into a few minutes earlier. As he made his way up the stairs he asked God to give him the strength and wisdom to make a just decision. Josh was sitting at the table pounding a baseball into his baseball glove. He didn't look up when his father entered.

"Mind if I sit down?"

"Why not," came the sarcastic reply, "It's your cabin isn't it?"

It was all Jake could do to hold his temper as he sat down across from Josh.

"Not really Josh, I had hoped it would be all of ours together."

The only reply that came out of Josh was a 'huh'.

"Why do you take such a hard stand on this when you don't really know what the school or baseball situation is here?"

"Oh really Pa. What kind of school or athletic program can you hope for in a dump like this?"

"Well for starters, the school you will be attending is at Price and it is a pretty big school, from what I hear," answered Jake.

Josh just sat there and shook his head and said nothing.

Jake stood up and walked around behind Josh and placed his hands on the top of Josh's chair. He was still upset with Josh's comments in the note he had written and decided he could not be silent about them any longer.

"I'm going to have my say Josh and you are going to sit there and listen whether you like it or not. Somewhere along the way someone has filled your head with the idea that you are good enough to play professional baseball. Maybe they're right and maybe someday you will be good enough for that, but I'll guarantee you that day hasn't arrived yet. You're sixteen years old, soon to be a Junior in high

57

school, and most importantly, you are my son and I am responsible for your well being. Soon enough you'll graduate from school and will probably walk out that door and do what you want to do."

Josh interrupted with, "You can count on that."

The comment riled Jake all the more and so he decided to lay it all on the line. In a voice Josh had never heard before, Jake continued.

"If you feel that way Josh then I'll be just as anxious as you are to slam that door behind you. When you get out there on your own you can make your own decisions, but until that day comes, you belong to me. So we're going to buy this place, you're going to work in the garage with me and learn a mechanic's trade and you're going to attend the school in Price. If they have a baseball program then good and if they don't, then tough."

Jake turned and walked toward the door. As he reached it, he stood there with his back to his son, pulled out a cigar and calmly lit it. He then turned and faced Josh.

"Might as well clear the air right here. In your note you said I owe you something. Well young man, I owe you nothing. I've given to your well being since the day you were born."

Jake put the cigar back in his mouth and returned to where Josh was sitting. He leaned on the table and looked his son right in the eyes from a distance of about a foot.

"When the day comes I owe you something, it'll be the day you've given something back for all these years of feeding, clothing and housing you. Until that day, I don't owe you doodlie-squat."

Jake turned and walked out the door, leaving Josh in silence.

Chapter Five

The war had entered its fourth year as the United States and its allies turned the tide of the war into their favor. The American people had rallied to the call of President Roosevelt. People from the dust bowl of the mid-west and the plains of Oklahoma migrated West to man the machinery in the war plants, building tanks, planes and the weapons needed by our men on the frontline. The slogan, 'One for all and all for one', echoed through the home front and rallied the American people around a common cause like never before in our country's history.

In the aftermath of a resounding defeat at the hands of the Japanese at Pearl Harbor, the country pulled together and showed the world what they were made of. The people suffered through their personal agony of war within their own families with the losses of sons and daughters. There was a shortage of commodities which gave way to rationing.

The road stop that was Thistle was evidence enough of a country at war. Sugar, tobacco and gasoline were just a few of the products being rationed by the government. If you used up your allotted stamps for the month then you went without that product until the next month. Jobs were plentiful but times were tough in some ways.

Jake had kept his promises after buying Thistle. What needed to be replaced was replaced and new paint was everywhere. New signs went up declaring the 'Canyon Garage' and 'The Sisters Café'. He was proud of it and so were Maggie and the kids.

Beth had a special teacher assigned to her to help with the trauma she experienced when she lost her mother. The report was she was progressing very well and was corresponding a lot better with other people. Yet, there always seemed to be that longing, empty look in her eyes.

Little Jake could not have been happier what with his two newly found possessions, a Schwynn bike and his own German Shepherd puppy, whom he named 'Babe', after the great Bambino, Babe Ruth. Of course the dog had grown considerable since Jake bought it home in his hat. The boy, the dog and the bike were inseparable from that day on.

Maggie was making good money as business was good and she saved what she could for the day she could return to Wheaton and bring her sisters back to Thistle to live with her. She figured another few months and she would be able to do it. She tried a few times to call home but all she got was a disconnect notice. However, the few times she called the café she was told her sisters were doing just fine.

As for Josh, well he still had his head in the clouds about playing baseball. However, things smoothed over between him and his father when school started and he found out that Price High School was top of the line in athletics. The real bonus for Josh was the coach, Allen Cross. Josh's bonus was turning out to be Jake's nightmare as the coach only fortified Josh's belief he was good enough to be a professional. For all the right reasons Jake accepted his son's interest in sports, mainly because Josh was a good student and agreed to help out in the garage and learn the mechanical skills his father was teaching him. Jake knew everything would go smoothly if the relationship remained on that basis, but somehow he knew the worst was yet to come.

Josh entered the café and took his usual seat at the counter. Maggie, in her usual up-beat fashion, placed a glass of water in front of him.

"What'll it be today Josh?"

"It's too hot to eat Maggie. I'll just have a chocolate sundae."

"Coming right up," Maggie answered.

As she was making the sundae, she spotted Little Jake approaching on his bike with Babe right on his heels. He had just finished his fourth year of school and he really cherished being with his dog and riding his bike now that summer vacation was here. He jumped off his bike and burst through the door with Babe almost knocking him down to get inside where it was cooler. Maggie was upset because he bought the dog into the café.

"Come on young man," she scolded. "You know the dog isn't allowed in here."

Little Jake pointed toward the door and commanded Babe.

"Outside Babe."

The dog immediately did an about face, pushed the screen door open with his nose, went outside and found some shade under the bench there. Little Jake jumped up on the stool next to Josh and asked for a coke.

"What's going on little brother?"

He reached into his pocket and pulled out a little four legged creature and placed it on the counter.

"Look what I found in my cave."

Maggie turned around just as the creature went under a napkin.

Now she was really upset.

"Get that lizard out of here," she yelled.

Little Jake laughed as he retreated the creature from under the napkin.

"That's not a lizard Maggie, it's a horned toad and it won't hurt you."

"Well it may not hurt me but it sure isn't good for business. So take your coke and horney toad and sit out on the bench with Babe."

Little Jake reluctantly picked up his critter and coke and went outside.

"Boy, that little brother of yours isn't afraid of anything out there, is he?"

"Yeah," answered Josh. "He's taken to the desert life like a fish to water. I sure don't see what he sees in a bunch of dirt and sage brush."

"Well, maybe he feels toward the desert like you feel towards baseball. He's learned a lot since he and the Indian boy, Chadego, became good friends. They spend a lot of time out there. Speaking of baseball, how are things going between you and your Pa?"

"Well, things are alright as long as I don't upset the schedule and that's what I'm worried about."

"Why, are you planning to upset the schedule?"

"Yea, I plan on making a big change for the coming school year."

Maggie leaned on the counter and put her chin in her hands and asked sympathetically, "Now what big change could you be making at Price High School?"

"That's just it Maggie, I don't want to go to Price next year. I want to go to school in Spanish Fork."

"You can't go to school there, you don't even live in Spanish Fork," she exclaimed.

"That's just it Maggie, I have a chance to live there with coach Cross's brother who is the coach of their baseball team. They've taken the championship two years running and pro scouts are always dropping by to take a look at the players."

Maggie was really surprised at what Josh had told her.

"You don't honestly believe your Pa is going to let you move to Spanish Fork do you?"

The excitement that had filled his face drained quickly away as he listened to her words. He knew she was right; Pa would never let him go somewhere else to school. Besides, Jake would have to hire someone to take his place in the garage. He looked at Maggie with a determined look.

"I'm going to ask him anyway. I have a right to ask, don't I?"

"Oh, you have the right to ask Josh but do me a favor. Let me know when you plan on doing the asking so I can be out of hearing range of your Pa."

Josh dejectedly began to eat his sundae knowing full well she was right. It would just turn into a shouting match between himself and his Pa. Oh well he thought, he would have all summer to ask so he wouldn't worry about it now.

A train whistle sounded from within the canyon, signaling another troop train going West. Its arrival always stirred things up in Thistle as it meant a busy time in the café and down at the tables set up at the depot. Maggie called to Beth across the room.

"Troop trains coming in Beth, better take the big pot of coffee down and set it up. I'll get Little Jake to bring the donuts."

Beth made her way from the café to the depot as the train whistled for the last crossing, and coming to a halt, bursts of steam bellowed from beneath her massive body. She sat the pot of coffee down on the table then took the donuts and sandwiches from Little Jake and readied them on platters.

She was proud to give some of her time to the boys going overseas, yet it saddened her to think that many would lose their lives or come home wounded. Because of these thoughts and the fresh memory of her mothers' death, she kept herself busy and rarely looked up. Little did she know the events of this day would change her life forever. Beth returned to tending to the troops. She suddenly realized that one young man had come around the table and was standing next to her.

"Beth", he said. "Beth Ritter, is that you?"

The mention of her name startled her as she straightened up and took a step backwards.

"It's me Beth, Jimmy Brant from Wheaton, Kansas."

It was only then that she recognized him as his uniform made him look older than she had remembered him. They had been close friends in high school, even though she was a freshman and he was a junior at the time. He had taken her to the Prom and it was because of leaving him she didn't want to move to California.

Her eyes seemed to sparkle as she threw her arms around him and embraced him. They hugged for a moment and then stood apart, facing each other, holding hands. They were a little embarrassed as the other troops began to whistle and make remarks, as only servicemen can.

"Alright you guys," Jim pleaded, "knock it off. She happens to be a good friend of mine from back home."

Of course they wouldn't let up so Jim took Beth's hand and led her away from the table to a more private spot.

"Gosh it's good to see you Beth, how have you been?"

"I've been fine Jimmy. It's so good to see you again."

He looked around for somewhere for them to sit. Beth, realizing what he wanted, took him by the hand and led him up the hill to the bench in front of the café. She noticed how strong his hand was and yet it held hers so gently. She was very excited, for it was the first time since her mother had died that she wanted to talk with someone.

He let go of her hand as they sat down but she reached for it again and held it tightly so he would know how glad she was to see him.

Maggie, seeing them through the window, recognized Jimmy and yelled back toward the kitchen.

"Albert, will you watch the front for a minute? I'm going outside."

"Yes mam," came the reply as he made his way through the kitchen door to the front.

Jake walked up to the café to get a cup of coffee as business was slow at the moment and, besides, he always liked to talk with the troops when the trains came in. He arrived in front of the café as Maggie came out the door. They both saw Beth standing with Jimmy Brant. Maggie hurried toward Jimmy as she extended her arms and embraced him.

"Jimmy Brant, is that really you?"

"Maggie, how are you and what are you doing here of all places?"

"I came here with Jake and the family. I own this café and Jake owns the rest of it. How is your family?"

"They're all fine Maggie."

She took him by the hand and led him back into the café and they all sat down at one of the tables.

"Come sit down and tell us all the news from home," she begged. "How were things in Wheaton when you left?"

The smile quickly left Jimmy's face as he looked around at each of them and then finally spoke.

"Wes Trembel died of a heart attack just before I enlisted in the army."

Maggie sat back in her chair and clasped her hands in her lap as she let the news sink in.

"That's why I haven't heard from him about my family lately. He would write to me every so often and tell me how they were doing. I called him when we decided to stay on here and he promised never to tell anyone where I was. Too bad, he was a good man and I'll miss him a lot."

She got up to go back to work but Jimmy took her by the arm and made her sit back down again.

"You better sit down Maggie because there's more bad news."

She looked very concerned as she returned to her chair.

Jimmy looked at Beth as he nervously toyed with his hat. He certainly did not want to be the bearer of bad news to his good friend.

"I'm sorry to be the one to tell you but your Ma and Pa are dead too."

Beth gasped as Maggie just stared at Jimmy in disbelief. Beth clutched Maggie's hand and began to cry. Maggie could only look at Jimmy, who was visibly shaken himself.

"How can they both be dead? What about my sisters?"

Jimmy looked away, wishing he weren't the one to relay such horrible news. He knew there was no getting out of it as he spoke very slowly and softly.

"Your sisters are fine. Your folks had gone to the Fourth of July picnic at the park. There was a lot of celebrating going on so when it got dark, a lot of the folks agreed to move the party over to the Anderson farm. Your Pa had too much too drink I guess and was driving too fast down the old levee road. Anyway, they missed the curve and slid off the road and into the water. The others finally found them after a long search but it was too late as both of them had drowned."

Maggie stood up and as she placed her hands to her face she made her way to the window. The room was silent as the others watched and waited for some reaction from her. Finally she turned and faced her friends and as she lifted her apron to wipe away her tears, she spoke.

"I'm sorry, but you've seen the only tears I'll ever shed for them. Do you know where my sisters are Jimmy?"

"Yes mam", he answered. "Your Aunt from Salt Lake City came to the funeral and took the girls back home with her. She asked everyone there to please notify her if your whereabouts became known. Of course, no one knew where you were."

Maggie stood in silence as she listened not knowing really what to say or do. Finally she composed herself enough to exit the room.

"If you'll excuse me now, I want to be alone for awhile."

She made her way past the group and went outside. They all watched as she made her way toward the cabin, walking at first and then running the last few yards. She entered the cabin and threw herself face first onto the bed with her head resting on the pillow. She put her hankie to her eyes and cried, "MaMa."

Meanwhile, back inside the café, Jimmy stood up and took Beth's hand, making her stand also.

"Look, Beth," he began, "I'm sorry for all the sad news I've brought here today. I was so happy to have found you again and now I've ruined even that. Please forgive me."

Beth hugged him to let him know everything was alright. In the distance the train whistle blew, calling the troops back to load up once again. They held their embrace.

"I've got to go now Beth. Walk me down to the train."

She broke away from him and found a piece of paper and pencil. She frantically wrote her address on it and handed it to Jimmy. He looked at what she had written.

"This is your address here and you want me to write to you?"

"Please Jimmy. Please write to me."

He led her outside and down the stairs and as they hurried along, hand in hand, it was as though they were kids again playing in the fields of home. They reached the platform where the troops were boarding the train. They stopped and faced each other standing hand in hand.

"Look Beth," he explained," I don't have a girl back home because I always considered you to be my girl. Would you be my girl again?"

"Yes, oh yes," she said excitedly as she threw her arms around his neck. As they stood back from the embrace he kissed her on the lips and she kissed him back.

"On the train, Brant," instructed the Sergeant.

Jimmy leaned forward and kissed her again and before she would open her eyes again he was boarding the train. Beth walked alongside the train as it slowly began its journey toward the canyon. Jimmy made his way to an open window and reached down and took her hands once again. She walked along the platform holding onto Jimmy's hand, and as the train picked up speed she soon reached the end of the platform where she was forced to let go of him. She stood there with tears in her eyes as Jimmy yelled back to her.

"I'll write to you Beth. Please write back to me. I'll be seeing you!"

Beth walked down the stairs at the end of the platform and waved goodbye as he and the train disappeared into the canyon. She wiped the tears from her eyes as the lonesome echo of the train whistle rang in her ears.

"Come back to me Jimmy Brant. God, please bring him back to me."

Little Jake, aware of his sister's sorrow, stood next to her with her hand in his as Babe sat by their side. Together the three of them turned and slowly made their way back toward the café. Beth turned and gave one last look down the tracks as the mournful sound of the whistle faintly echoed one last time.

Ж

The following weeks found the Ritter family and Maggie deeply involved in their work. The little canyon stop was abuzz with activity and yet, as busy as it was, it seemed that each of them was working toward their own goals.

Beth had received numerous letters from Jimmy who, by now, had seen much combat. Each letter, received or sent, seemed to solidify their relationship. The height of her day was the mail delivery.

Little Jake was given a Red Ryder BB gun for his birthday by his Pa and so he felt there was nothing else he would ever need in his lifetime. He and his Indian friend, Chadego, were becoming tuned into the land around them and each seemed to learn the other's ways and customs. More importantly, they learned to respect each other's customs and beliefs and so together worked to respect the land. Little did they know then their relationship would set a course for them that would be their future.

Little Jake was happiest when the chores were done so he and Babe could go to the cave he had discovered a few yards behind the row of cabins. He had dug little shelves into the walls and placed candles on them for better lighting. He had talked his Pa out of an old stuffed chair and table which he set up in one corner of the cave. On the other side he laid down an old mattress from one of the cabins where he would lay with Babe when he read his comic books. At that point in his life he knew there was nothing in California he would ever need for he had become one with the land that was Thistle.

Josh was learning the mechanical skills his father was taking the time to teach him and even he had to admit to himself it was very interesting.

When he wasn't working in the garage he spent his spare time down by the old shed where he rigged up a wooden frame, the size of the strike zone for batters. He spent hours just throwing baseballs through it, sharpening his control. Of course, the project went a lot smoother when his Pa made him hang a mattress behind the frame so everyone wouldn't have to listen to the balls crashing against the side of the shed. He was anxious for school to begin again so he could get back to playing baseball.

He was not, however, looking forward to confronting his father on the issue of attending his senior year in Spanish Fork. He dreaded that day but he knew full well that day would have to be soon if arrangements were to be made.

Maggie did not allow herself to grieve very long about the loss of her parents. She didn't know if it was because of the way she was treated at home or because she was channeling all her thoughts and energy into making sure her sisters were alright.

Whatever the reason, for the first time in her life she felt free and unafraid. She had called her Aunt Edna in Salt Lake City and, after a lengthy conversation with her, was able to talk with her sisters.

Having them join her in Thistle was nearer to becoming a reality now as the old house in Wheaton was sold and she and her brothers were to split the money three ways. She knew it would only be a matter of time before they would all be reunited once again.

Ж

Jake entered the café and occupied his usual stool by the cash register. Maggie finished clearing off a table and then hurriedly made her way over to where Jake was sitting. She was all aglow and smiling which Jake recognized immediately.

"Well, aren't you a picture of joy today?"

"Oh Jake, I'm so happy today. I called my Aunt in Salt Lake City and she wants me to come and visit them this week if possible or as soon as I can. Isn't that great?"

"Well, I'm glad for you Maggie but how's about a cup of coffee for a paying customer?"

"Oh, I'm sorry Jake," she said as she reached for the coffee pot. "It's just that I'm so excited."

Jake sipped his coffee as he listened to her go on about her sisters.

"Well, how are your sisters doing anyway?"

"Oh, they're doing just fine Jake, for now, but they want to come here and live with me."

Jake mulled that over in his mind as he stirred his coffee. Everything seemed to be moving at a fast rate of speed lately, not only with Maggie and her family, but with his own family. He was not one who liked sudden changes that might disrupt the operation of Thistle.

"That's a pretty big order, isn't it?"

"It is right now but I've been going over the books and I think in about six months I can swing it."

"So, are you planning to go see your aunt this week?"

"I'd like to go this weekend if I can get Jeannie to cover for me for a few days."

Jake finished his coffee, laid fifteen cents on the counter and made his way toward the door.

"Not much of a tip big spender," she teased.

Without turning to face her he answered her.

"If I leave a big tip you'll always expect a big tip."

She smiled as she closed the door behind him. He made his way back to the garage area where he was working on a 1940 Buick. He had no sooner resumed working when a young man approached holding a brief case in one hand and his hat in the other. He wore a suit but appeared to be sweaty and disheveled.

"Excuse me, mister, do run this garage?"

"Yep, sure do," Jake answered as he continued to work on the car. "You have car problems?"

The man withdrew a handkerchief from his pocket and began wiping his brow.

"Yes, I broke down about two miles down the road. Something went out and I can't get it started. I had to walk to get here in this heat."

"What kind of car do you have?"

"It's a black 1942 Lincoln and it's parked on the side of the road about a mile or so east of here.

Jake looked at the man and, from his appearance, couldn't help but smile.

"Well, you're a mess", Jake observed. "Tell you what. Why don't you wash up in the men's room over there and then go into the café and get something to eat. In the meantime I'll send my son with the tow truck to fetch your car. We'll take a look at it and find out what the matter is. Just leave the keys with me."

"Sounds good to me. Which way did you say the men's room was?"

Jake pointed in the direction of the room.

"Right down there, first door on the left. The café is just around the corner."

He thanked Jake and made his way toward the room.

Ж

Maggie noticed him right away as he made his way to a small table in the corner. After all, it wasn't too often she had customers come in wearing a suit and carrying a briefcase. She waited a moment, and then made her way to his table with a glass of water and a menu. Without looking up he took the menu and opened it.

"How are you doing today?" she asked.

Still looking at the menu and without looking up he answered.

"I've had better days."

Realizing his mood, she politely said she'd return in a minute to take his order. Without looking up he answered.

"Ya, alright."

He scanned the menu and laid it down on the table. More composed now, he surveyed the room. When he looked at Maggie their eyes met and he instantly looked down hoping she was not the waitress waiting on him knowing how cold he had been to her.

He didn't have time to think on it further as Maggie was now standing at his table, check pad in hand. She was smiling at him.

"Are you ready to order now or would you like more time to ponder your rotten day?"

He looked up and saw that beautiful face smiling at him. He looked very sheepish and embarrassed.

"That bad, huh?" he asked.

"Oh, not too bad. I've seen worse but then there's nothing that says you have to be happy when you sit down to eat."

"I'm sorry. I've had a rotten day so far. My car broke down; I'm all sweaty, tired and hungry."

She was glad to see him in a better mood.

"No need to be sorry. Now, I can take care of the hungry part but tired and sweaty are up to you, so what'll you have?"

He glanced at the menu again and answered.

"Oh, the special I guess."

"Good choice," she answered. She turned and made her way to the counter, using every smooth move she could muster without being too obvious. It must have worked because after she called in the order she looked over in his direction and he was still watching her. They both smiled.

In the meantime, Jake had sent Josh to tow the car into the garage. It took about an hour to retrieve it and for Jake to locate the problem. Maggie came by the stranger's table with the coffee for the third time.

"Oh no," he insisted, "I don't think I can swallow another drop, but thank you anyway."

"You're really in a fix, aren't you?"

"I guess so." He replied. "I'm supposed to be in Salt Lake City the day after tomorrow at a very important meeting. It has to do with a government contract I just bid on recently."

"Oh, you're a salesman or something?" she asked.

"You might say that," he answered with a smile on his face. "I own a tool and die company in Salt Lake."

Jake entered the café and located the table where his client was sitting. He made his way to the table, clip board in hand and began talking.

"Doesn't look good young fella. Looks like the carburetor is way out of whack."

"How long will it take to fix?" came the reply.

"Oh, could have the part tomorrow if they don't have to order it and have your car for you by Friday noon."

"Well, it's got to be fixed so go ahead with it. Is there some way I can get to Salt Lake from here?"

"Yes," answered Jake. "There's a train coming through here at seven in the morning. In the meantime, we have cabins in the back if you care to get a good night's rest and take a shower."

"Sounds good to me." came his enthusiastic reply.

He pulled out his wallet and handed Jake his business card. Jake placed it on the clipboard along with the work order. He read the business card.

Wallace Tool and Die Co.
Edmond Wallace – Owner
1471 Briscomb Ave.
Salt Lake City, Utah
Ph. 544-1771

"Ok Mr. Wallace, I'll get right on this for you. Maggie here will get you all set up for a room. Hope you enjoy your stay."

"Well, Mr. Wallace, are you ready to see your cabin?" Maggie asked.

"Oh please Maggie, call me Edmond." he said.

She smiled as she spoke.

"Yes. Well, Edmond, when you're finished just come over to the cash register and I'll give you the key to your cabin."

Edmond nodded as he finished his coffee. He sat there a moment contemplating his plight. He would get to Salt Lake alright but how would he get his car back? Oh well, he thought, at least I can get a good nights sleep and think about the rest in the morning. He made his way to the counter where Maggie was talking with Little Jake who was sipping on a coke.

"This your boy?" asked Edmond.

"Oh, no," she was quick to reply. "This is Jake's youngest son, Little Jake. I'm not married."

A smile crossed his lips as she answered.

"Me neither, I guess I never found the time."

"Yes. If you'll just fill out the registration card I'll have this young man show you to your cabin."

He filled out the card and took the key from Maggie.

"Come on young man, lead the way."

Maggie stood and watched as the two of them left the café and made their way toward the cabins. Edmond followed along as Little Jake and Babe played fetch with a stick along the way. She didn't know exactly what it was about Mr. Wallace, she only knew she felt good all over when she was around him.

Ж

Jake had sent Josh to Price for the parts to Edmond's car. Josh parked his truck in front of the parts store and made his way to the entrance. As he reached the door a familiar voice called out his name.

"Hey Josh, wait up," commanded the voice.

Josh looked down the street to see Coach Cross making his way toward him. Josh wished the coach hadn't seen him for he knew what question the coach was going to ask him; however, it was too late.

"Coach Cross, how are you doing?"

"Oh I'm fine Josh. The question is how are you doing? Have you been practicing like I asked you to do?"

Together they entered the store.

"Sure coach, I've been throwing every day working on my control and I feel really good."

"That's great Josh. Have you asked your father about attending Spanish Fork High School next year?"

Josh's hesitation in answering the question only made him more uneasy with the situation. Coach Cross didn't wait for an answer.

"You haven't asked him yet, have you?"

Josh shook his head no and looked away.

"It can't be that hard to do. Your dad would be a fool to say no to an opportunity like this for you."

Josh squirmed a bit as he answered the coach.

"Ya but you don't know my Pa. He doesn't think too highly of my playing baseball."

"Would it help if I asked him for you Josh?" the coach replied.

"No, no. I'll ask him when I get back today."

Coach saw it was upsetting Josh to talk about it so he backed off.

"Tell you what Josh, you go back and ask your father and if he says no to the idea, give me a call and I'll drop by the garage and have a talk with him on your behalf."

"That's fine coach, I'll let you know."

Coach Cross made his way out of the store and down the street, leaving Josh to wonder why playing baseball had to be such a stressful thing. He wished he were old enough to make his own decisions. He wished he could just play baseball and forget about what his father thought and putting all those hours in a garage. Most of all, he didn't want to face his father with the idea of going to school somewhere else.

Josh was in no hurry to return to Thistle so he drove slower than normal, biding his time to think out his strategy. He knew one thing, as he pulled the truck into the garage area where his father was waiting for him, time had run out and the time to ask was today. As he entered the office he could tell Jake was a little upset with him.

"Well, you made it back," said Jake. "I was beginning to wonder if you had broken down or something. Did you get the part?"

"Ya Pa, here it is. Sorry I took so long. I ran into Coach Cross at the parts store and we got to talking baseball."

Jake was going through some papers and after sorting through them returned some of them to the safe. He had a worried look on his face as he locked the safe. Josh noticed the look but decided to ask his father's permission to change schools.

"Pa, I've got something I want to talk to you about. It's important."

Jake gathered up some papers from the desk and headed for the door.

"Well it's going to have to wait until later Josh. I've got a man from the state highway department waiting for me in the café. You're going to have to watch the station until we finish our business."

"But Pa, this is important to me."

"And this is important to me so it's just going to have to wait until I'm finished," he answered as he went out the door.

Josh pounded his fist on the table. "Damn him."

Jake made his way over to the café and sat down at the table where his visitor was just finishing his meal.

"Sorry to make you wait Mr. Wentz, I had to wait for my son to return from Price."

"Oh that's alright Mr. Ritter. I really enjoyed the meal. You really have a nice establishment here."

"Thank you. We think so too," Jake replied.

Maggie came to the table with a pot of coffee in hand.

"You gentlemen care for a cup of coffee?" she asked.

"That would be nice," acknowledged Mr. Wentz. "I'll take a piece of that apple pie in the case also."

Jake leaned back in his chair and took a sip of coffee as he waited for Maggie to bring the pie. He was a little nervous not knowing the nature of Wentz's business.

"Well Mr. Wentz, what brings you to Thistle?"

He reached down and picked up his briefcase from the floor beside his chair. He opened it and rummaged through its contents, finally pulling out a variety of paperwork.

"I'll get right to the point, Mr. Ritter. The way things are going the war will be over soon and the big boys up at the state capital are getting ready to put into action a plan to do much needed repairs and construction on our highway system."

"Well, that's a good deal," said Jake. "This road could use some fixing."

Wentz pulled a large map from his briefcase and spread it out on the table, facing it toward Jake.

"I'm afraid it's not as simple as that, Mr. Ritter. The road through this canyon has always been a thorn in the highway department's side, what with the washouts during the heavy rains and grading during the snowy season."

"There haven't been any washouts or snow removal trouble since I've been here," said Jake.

Wentz took another bite of pie and a sip of coffee before he answered.

"You are right about that but you must remember the past few years have been classified as drought years and we've been very fortunate."

"So, you build a better road. What's the problem?" asked Jake.

"If you'll follow along with me on the map I'll point out our situation. You see, you're situated right smack dab in the middle of the canyon with an opening at either end. Going either way from Thistle the railroad stays on the canyon floor and follows the creek. The highway makes its way to higher ground, which is solid rock on one side with railway and creek on the other. Now the department is currently studying two plans to make this portion of the road safer and more economically feasible."

Jake sat in silence and studied the map as Wentz pulled yet another map from the briefcase and placed it on top of the other one and Wentz continued to explain.

"Now this is a detailed map the surveyors have drawn up which shows just the portion of the highway as it comes through Thistle. This is plan A and, if you will note, for it to be implemented we would have to widen the existing road. To do that we would be taking at least twenty feet of your property facing the existing road."

Jake pulled the map closer to him and scanned it.

"But that puts the roadway just five feet from my gas pumps. I won't have any access or parking available. It also takes away most of the parking for the café."

He stood up and leaned across the table as he spoke to Wentz.

"What the hell you people trying to do, put me out of business?"

"Now Mr. Ritter, don't get upset. We're not trying to put you out of business."

Jake leaned over the map once again. He was very emotional now and very upset at the plan presented to him.

"Why can't you move the road toward the tracks? There's plenty of room there for that."

"We can't do that." exclaimed Wentz. "The railroad owns fifty feet on either side of the tracks; that's their right-of-way."

"Well, I own the frontage from the existing road to my businesses. Doesn't that count for anything?"

"Oh we're aware of your property lines Mr. Ritter and the state will make you a fair offer for the property needed to expand the road. That is, of course, if this plan is the one to be implemented."

"Excuse me a minute." said Jake.

He turned and made his way over to the coffee pot where Maggie was standing.

"What's the matter Jake? You look pretty mad?" she asked.

"Damn right I'm mad," he shot back. "That Wentz fellow from the highway department tells me we're going to have to give up our frontage road so they can widen the highway."

The comment startled Maggie.

"You're kidding. What are you going to do?"

"I don't know yet. There's one more plan I haven't seen yet so I'll have to let you know."

Jake walked back to the table and sat down, a little calmer now than when he left. He apologized for the interruption and waited for the next presentation.

"Oh, that's alright Mr. Ritter. I have all the time in the world; however, you'll find you don't."

"What does that mean?" Jake shot back.

Wentz reached into his briefcase and pulled out yet another map and placed it on the table in front of a very upset Jake.

"This is Plan B which is also being considered by our department. Now, you'll notice, this plan calls for a new route through the canyon. In fact it will bypass Thistle all together as it follows a higher ground. It will start at the south end of the canyon and meet up at the north end of the existing road."

Jake stood up again and, trying to control his temper, let the words come out through clinched teeth.

"You know damn well this plan will by-pass my business."

Wentz leaned back in his chair and put a toothpick into his mouth he had in his vest pocket and calmly answered Jake.

"It most certainly would sir, however, it would not effect the existing road in front of your property and that seems to be what you are most concerned about."

Maggie, realizing Jake's temper was getting the best of him, went over to the table and asked if everything was alright. Wentz began replacing the maps back into his briefcase.

Jake threw his hands up into the air as he ranted and raved about how the highway department was going to put them out of business. He finally leaned on the table again and hotly spoke to Mr. Wentz.

"Listen you little pipsqueak, you go on back and tell your bosses I'll fight these plans even if it means going to the governor's office."

Wentz stood up, placed the money for the meal on the table and looked at the both of them.

"You are evidently very upset so I don't feel we should carry on this conversation any longer. If you'll please excuse me, I'll be on my way."

Jake walked with him as he made his way to the door.

"You're damn right I'm upset Wentz, and I'll tell you this, I'm going to Salt Lake and get to the bottom of this."

Wentz stopped at the door and answered Jake.

"That's a very good idea Mr. Ritter. In fact, if you'll be at the Department of Highway's main office on Friday of this week you can voice your opinion to a three man panel. They will be deciding which plan to be implemented.

"And just what time will that be messenger boy?"

"One thirty sharp, Mr. Ritter."

"Well, I'll be there with bells on and I hope the hell you'll be there because I'm going to tell that panel what great pleasure you get out of destroying someone's dream by ruining their business."

"You know Mr. Ritter, you should learn to control your temper. I have found through my experiences in dealing with people, that a lot more can be accomplished where cooler heads prevail. Too bad sir, you're probably a very good mechanic but you are a lousy businessman."

Jake spun around and slammed his fist on the table so hard the sugar and napkin holder went flying off the table.

"That son-of-a-bitch." he yelled.

Josh saw Jake coming toward him from the café and it didn't take too long to figure out his Pa was really mad about something. He stood up from his seat at the desk as Jake entered the office and began swearing and hollering about the stupid highway department and how they were going to put them out of business.

Josh just stood there in awe of Jake's temper. He couldn't recall ever seeing him so upset. He tried to ask Jake what the matter was but he just kept rambling on as he pulled papers from the safe. Finally he blurted out a question.

"What's the matter Pa?"

"What's the matter? What's the matter? We're about to lose this whole operation if they have their way. Well, I'll tell you this, they're not going to get away with it. I'll take them to court if I have to."

Now Josh was a little upset also. What if that meant they would have to move away from Thistle to God knows where.

"What do you mean lose this place? What did they do?"

Jake continued to open and slam drawers as if he were looking for something. Finally, in the back of the bottom drawer of the desk, he found what he was looking for, a pint of whisky. He sat back down in the chair, took the cap off the bottle and took a swig.

Josh was taken by surprise because he never saw his father drink before. He just stood there with that astonished look of disbelief on his face.

Jake looked over at his son and upon seeing that look on his face became very sarcastic.

"What's the matter, never seen a man drink before?"

Josh couldn't believe what he was seeing and hearing.

"Yes, I've seen people drink before, but never my father."

Jake slumped down in the chair and stared at the bottle for a moment.

"Well, I'm damn well old enough to drink so why don't you run along and throw some more baseballs at the shed."

Josh whirled around and went out the door wondering what all this meant for all of them. He did know, however, that the frame of mind Jake was in there would be no opportunity to ask about changing schools. His thoughts were swirling in his head as he made his way across the dirt. He wondered when he would be able to ask his father about changing schools and what he would tell Coach Cross or could he even face him? He just wanted to find a place to hide and maybe everything would go away, like a bad dream.

Chapter Six

Maggie was awakened by the screams coming from Beth's room. She ran into Beth's room to find her sitting straight up in bed screaming "Mama, Mama". Maggie wrapped her arms around her and tried to console her. Beth finally stopped crying and buried her head in Maggie's chest.

"It's alright sweetheart, it's just one of your nightmares again," Maggie assured her.

"It was different this time Maggie," Beth answered, sobbing heavily.

"How was it different honey?"

"I saw things I've never seen before. This time I saw a small explosion and then the fire while Mama was in the house getting her garden gloves. I began screaming for her to come out and as the dream ended I saw a figure running from the front of the house toward a truck. That's when I woke up screaming."

"Did you see who the person was or what the truck looked like?' asked Maggie.

"No, it all happened so fast and it was the first time I've seen all that."

Maggie stood up and placed her hand on Beth's shoulder. She was concerned at how often Beth was having these attacks. The doctor said she would keep on having them until the whole sequence of events was revealed to her. Her sub-conscience mind was coming alive when she slept.

"I'm going to get dressed and go to work now but I think you will be alright."

Beth lay back on the bed and tried to relax. She couldn't help but wonder who the person was fleeing from the front of the house. It was the first time that had been revealed to her and could that person be the one who set the fire? She was exhausted from it all and fell asleep once more, this time into a deep sleep.

Sometime later in the day there was a knock on her door that woke her up. She went to the door and opened it to see Little Jake standing there with a big grin on his face.

"There's a letter for you Sister and it's from Jimmy."

The thought of a letter from Jimmy lifted her spirits greatly. She reached for the letter and thanked her little brother for bringing it to her. The excitement grew within her as she clutched the letter to her bosom. As was her ritual, when she received a letter from him, she went to the phonograph and placed their record on it and turned it on. It was their record because she and Jimmy agreed the song, "I'll Be Seeing You", would always be their song. As the music began to fill the room she sat in her chair, opened the letter and began to read.

My Dearest Beth;

"Today I received three letters from you as my mail finally caught up with me. You'll never know how much your writing has meant to me and what impact it has made on me in surviving this terrible war.

Your words fill me with the realization of why we're fighting this war, in an effort to kill this beast that is Hitler and his army. A day hasn't gone by that I don't remember holding you in my arms and kissing you good-by the day we parted. That moment in my life has served as a reminder of all that is good and worth fighting for in this world. In all honesty, finding you again has pulled me through a time in my life I would like to forget.

The fact is sweetheart, I will be fighting no longer as I am writing this letter from a hospital bed somewhere in Europe. As I write this letter to you the doctors are deciding on whether to take my right leg or try to save it. As you read this letter, that decision will already have been made.

I ask that you don't cry for me because I'm not crying for me. I'm lucky to be alive either way and the most important thing is that I'm going to be coming home as soon as I am able. My only thoughts now are of you and what beautiful things lay ahead for us. That is, of course, if you feel as I do about us.

I'll close for now and say so long. I'll be seeing you sweetheart...... soon."

All My Love

Jim

P.S. "Thanks for the cookies. My buddies and I finished them off."

Beth pressed the letter to her face as tears made their way down her cheeks and onto the letter.

"Please God, save his leg and bring him home soon."

Jake had already made his way to the café and was enjoying his breakfast and coffee. He sat at his usual place at the counter enjoying the quiet of the morning before he had to face the hustle and bustle of a new day. He loved what he had created at Thistle and was very proud of all the accomplishments along the way.

His children had a good home and were getting a good education; Maggie was doing very well operating the café and, most important to him, he was finally doing something with his life he enjoyed doing.

Whenever he allowed his thoughts to wander back to his days on the farm, it sent a chill up his back. He so detested working the land which required so many long hours each day, working under conditions so contrary to his liking.

Having dwelled on those years briefly, he would quickly bring himself back to the comfort of a good cup of coffee and the surroundings he built his dream on. For Jake, it was enough to know that Thistle was his, and, for better or worse, he commanded all of it for he was the boss.

Yet, for all that he had accomplished, it was apparent to him now that he could lose it all if the highway was to bypass Thistle. A new highway on higher ground would make Thistle an off-ramp stop only. As he sipped his coffee it was comforting for him to know that tomorrow he would be at a meeting in Salt Lake where he could present his case to the entire board and not just arrogant Mr. Wentz.

Maggie came from the kitchen area and was putting on her apron as she walked toward where Jake was sitting. She no sooner had arrived when the phone rang so she reached over and answered it.

"Sisters café", she announced.

"Yes, is Jake Ritter there please?"

"Yes, he's sitting right here, hang on a second please."

"Is that you Maggie?" the man asked.

"Yes it is and who is this?"

"This is Edmond in Salt Lake and I'm calling about my car."

"Well good morning Edmond and how are you this morning?" she answered as her excitement level quickened.

"I'm fine thank you. Let me speak to Jake and then I would love to talk to you after I've spoken with him."

"Oh sure, here he is." She replied.

She motioned to Jake to come to the phone and when she handed him the phone he noticed she had a big grin on her face.

"It's Edmond Wallace in Salt Lake calling about his car."

He placed his hand over the mouthpiece as he spoke to Maggie.

"How come you're so excited, he's calling me about the car?"

"Yes, but he wants to talk to me after he talks to you so hurry up and talk.

"This is Jake, how may I help you?"

"Good morning Jake, this is Edmond and I was wondering if my car is ready yet?"

"She's all fixed and ready to roll sir,"came Jake's reply.

"That's good news," he answered. "All I have to do now is make arrangements to get it."

Jake thought a second before answering.

"Well, if you're too busy to come and get it I would be glad to bring it to you tomorrow, if that's convenient for you."

"Oh I wouldn't impose on you like that Mr. Ritter."

"It's no big deal sir. I have to be in Salt Lake tomorrow on business anyway."

"Yes but how will you get back to Thistle?" he asked.

"That's no problem; I'll just take the train back. I love riding the train."

"Well that's very kind of you Jake, that'll save me a trip. Of course I'll pay all expenses, just add it to my bill."

"Will do sir." Jake replied.

"Now you have my address at work on the card I left with you and I'll be there waiting for you, say around ten o'clock?"

"That will be just fine." Jake agreed.

"Could I speak with Maggie for just a second?"

"Sure, hold on just a minute."

Jake put his hand over the mouthpiece as he handed the phone to Maggie.

"He wants to talk with you. Probably wants to ask you for a date."

"Just give me the phone smarty; he just wants to talk to me."

"This is Maggie."

"Yes Maggie. Jake is bringing my car to me tomorrow and I was wondering if you might like to come with him? I sure would like to show you around the town."

She was doing her best to conceal the excitement in her voice as she answered.

"I'd like that very much. It would be a great chance for me to see my sisters if you wouldn't mind dropping me off at my Aunt's house?"

"Well, I'll do better than that Maggie, I'll go with you and after your visit we can spend some time together; if that's alright with you?"

"That's fine with me Edmond, but do you think you'll have time for all that, what with your busy schedule?"

"Hey, I'm the boss remember? Besides, I need to get away from here for awhile."

She was all aglow as she answered softly.

"Well, if it's alright with you it sounds great to me."

"Then it's settled. I'll see you around ten tomorrow."

"Thank you Edmond. Good-by."

She hung up the phone and began jumping up and down, giggling all the while. Jake put down his coffee cup and watched in amazement as Maggie did her little dance. Finally, he could contain himself no longer.

"What the Hell are you so happy about?"

She danced her way over to where Jake was sitting. She placed her elbows on the table and propped her chin in her hands and answered.

"Well, if you must know Mr. Smarty Pants, Mr. Wallace wants me to come with you tomorrow to Salt Lake when you return his car. Then he's going to take me over to my Aunt Edna's house to see the girls. Oh, Jake isn't that wonderful, I'll be with my sisters again?"

Jake recognized her happiness for he knew what her sisters meant to her and he didn't want to ruin the moment. He took her hands in his and looked her in the eyes as he answered.

"That's great Maggie and I'm really happy for you."

Her eyes welled up with tears as she thanked him. Not wanting to leave it on a crying note, he stood up and placed some money on the counter and then walked toward the door.

"Better be careful Maggie. Those rich guys have a way of sweeping young girls off their feet with kindness when all they really want is their bodies."

The dish rag hit the door as it closed, and as he made his way toward the garage he could hear her yelling something about "He's not that kind of man" and "What does a grease monkey know anyway?" He smiled as he lit up a cigar and just stood there surveying all that was his. This was Thistle, his dream, his life and no one was going to take it from him.

Ж

Jake pulled the Lincoln around to the front of Maggie's cabin and honked the horn. When she didn't respond he honked it all the more and was mumbling something to the effect about how slow women were and never on time.

Finally she appeared and made her way to the car. Of course, when she got in, he was still mumbling about being late; however, she just ignored him. No one or anything was going to ruin this day for her. Jake drove across the gravel parking lot and onto the highway and the two of them headed for Salt Lake City. Neither of them could possibly know what the day's events would bring for them.

Maggie was very excited about the thought of seeing her sisters again. Then, of course, there was the excitement of being with Edmond again. All in all she had great expectations for having a great time.

Jake, on the other hand, was in a very somber mood and Maggie sensed it. She was well aware of the importance of this meeting between Jake and the Highway Department. The outcome would not only determine the fate of Thistle but could forever change their lives. Knowing this to be true, she couldn't help but approach Jake with the question.

"Jake, what will we do if they vote to bypass Thistle?"

He was quick to answer as he had been mulling the same question over and over in his own mind.

"I don't know Maggie but if that's their decision we're in a heap of hurt."

"Didn't Mr. Wentz say that if they build on higher ground it was possible they could also build a new on and off ramp for Thistle?"

"Oh sure, that would be just great for business. We're located between Price and Spanish Fork, which are fairly good sized towns. People will stop to eat there and gas up so they won't have to leave the main highway on their way to Salt Lake. Our business will see a drastic reduction in revenue and that's a fact."

Content in her own mind that Jake had answered the question she dropped the subject. She didn't want to get him all steamed up before he got to the meeting. She needed to tell Jake about Beth's reoccurring nightmares.

"I've been meaning to tell you about Beth's bad dreams. She has them more frequently now."

"Well, the doctor said that would happen." replied Jake.

"Yes I know, but they are getting more frightening each time. The last one she had was about the fire, as usual, but this time she saw someone running away from the front of the house towards a truck."

Jake seemed a little startled at what she had told him. He composed himself quickly, however, and answered very calmly.

"It's too bad she has to go through all this. Did she say who the person was running to the truck?"

"No, the dream happened so fast and ended so quickly she didn't have time to recognize any one."

"Well, you know Maggie, these are just nightmares and who knows what will come up? This could all be a figment of her imagination. Even if she recognizes the person, if there really was one, you can't base any facts on it because it just isn't real."

Maggie was a little upset at Jake's attitude and he could tell in her response she didn't agree with him.

"Well, it's very real for Beth and I would think you would be very interested in what she was experiencing. It might answer a lot of questions about the fire."

"Well fine, if she comes up with a face then we will address it. Until then, it's just speculation so let's drop it, o.k.?"

"I'm just trying to help Jake. You don't have to get so upset."

"You are Maggie and I'm sorry. It's just that I have all these other important matters on my mind and I just don't have the time to deal with Beth's problem right now. I'll have a talk with her when I get back, o.k.?"

"Do what you want Jake, she's your daughter."

She laid her head back on the headrest and closed her eyes. Jake looked over to see her get comfortable and then brought his eyes back to the road. He was glad she didn't have any more questions concerning Beth or the fate of Thistle, questions he really didn't have any answers for.

Maggie sat straight up as the car came to a complete halt and Jake shut the motor off. She was unfamiliar with the surroundings of course.

"Are we in Salt Lake already?" she asked.

"Yes, we're downtown but you have a couple of miles to go yet. Here, I've drawn you a map and it's really simple to get to Edmond's place of business. Just follow Temple Street for about a mile until you come to West fifty-fourth. Hang a right there and drive until you come to Briscomb Lane. Turn left and his business is at 1471 in the first block."

"How did you find all that out?" she asked surprisingly.

"Easy." he replied. "I just got out a map of Salt Lake last night and wrote down all the information for you."

He started to get out of the car but she grabbed his arm and pulled him back inside.

"Thanks for everything Jake." she said.

Before he could answer, she leaned over and kissed him on the cheek.

"Good luck today Jake."

Jake seemed taken back by her sudden show of affection but his mind wasn't tuned into her at the moment. He placed his hand on hers.

"Good luck to you too, Maggie."

She watched as he made his way up the stairs of the Highway Department building and went inside. Once he disappeared, she pulled the car into the traffic flow and went West on Temple Street. Once again her thoughts turned to Edmond and her sisters. She couldn't believe that on this day all she had dreamed of and worked for would come true.

She glanced at the map Jake had given her and made a right turn onto 54th street. About three blocks up from where she turned she saw Briscomb Lane and turned left. Sure enough, there was the entrance gate to "Wallace Tool and Die Company". Her heart quickened as she stopped at the entrance guard shack. A guard came over to her window as she rolled her window down.

"Good morning miss, is there something I can help you with?

"I'm returning Mr. Wallace's car to him. I believe he's expecting me."

"One moment miss, I'll call his office for instructions," he replied.

He returned to the shack and picked up the telephone. She sat there patiently and was in awe at the size of Edmond's company and was very impressed with Mr. Wallace's accomplishments. The guard returned to her car and handed her a "Visitor Badge."

"Mr. Wallace is expecting you. Please wear this badge in plain sight at all times. If you'll proceed to the office complex, across the way, and park in Mr. Wallace's parking spot, he'll be there to meet you."

"Thank you so much." she answered.

"You're welcome miss."

She pulled away and drove to the parking area where she found the correct parking space and eased the Lincoln into place. Edmond appeared at the railing surrounding a small flight of stairs and greeted her.

"Hi Maggie, how are you today?"

She opened the door and got out of the car as she answered.

"I'm fine Edmond."

"It's good to see you again. Come on up and we'll go to my office."

She made her way to the top of the stairs and was expecting him to open the door but he just stood there smiling.

"What's the matter?" she asked.

"I guess I'll just have to call security and have you apprehended." he said jokingly. "You don't have a visitor's badge on."

"Oh, I'm sorry Edmond. I put it in my purse by mistake. It's because I'm really excited about being in Salt Lake today."

She retrieved it from her bag and attached it to her blouse.

"That's better," he said as he opened the door for her. "Wouldn't want to lose you so soon after waiting so long to see you again."

Maggie was pleasantly surprised by his comment and as they walked down the hallway past many more offices she asked, "why all the security?"

"Well, most of our contracts are for the government and to work here one needs a security clearance. Each of my employees wears a badge identifying his or her security clearance status. With a visitor's badge, such as yours, you are only allowed in non-restricted areas, such as my office."

He opened his office door and bid her to enter. He motioned to a chair at the desk for her to sit in as he made his way to his own chair on the other side.

"Excuse me a moment." he said as he pushed a button on the intercom on his desk.

"Lori, hold all my calls until I come out."

"Yes Mr. Wallace," she answered.

When he turned to talk with Maggie, the sight of her made him realize she was prettier than he had remembered.

"So Maggie how is everything with you?"

"Oh I'm just fine Edmond. I'm very excited about seeing my sisters again. I want to thank you for letting me bring your car to you. It saved Jake and I a little money on train tickets."

"Don't thank me Maggie. I should be thanking you for returning it to me. It saved me a trip to Thistle and enabled me to finish my business for the week."

He rose from his chair and circled the desk where he sat on the end of it next to her.

"To show my appreciation, I'd love to take you to lunch."

Maggie was a little embarrassed that he would ask her out for lunch. It wasn't that she didn't want to go, she just couldn't think of anything more important to her than seeing her sisters again. She stood up and faced him.

"I would really love to go to lunch with you Edmond but I'll have to make it another time I think. I told my Aunt I would be at her house around eleven and I'm sure she is expecting me to be on time."

He stood up as she stood up and faced her as he took her hands in his.

"Of course, how stupid of me. Tell you what Maggie, I'm through for the week anyway so what do you say I drive you over to see your sisters and after that we can decide what we want to do?"

He motioned her toward the door and as they exited the office she answered him.

"That's very nice of you Edmond but I don't want to take up any of your time waiting for me. If you would just drop me off at my Aunt's house that would be fine."

"Nonsense Maggie, we'll just make a day of it. Besides, I'd love to meet the whole family and if it means being with you then all the better."

Maggie couldn't believe what she was hearing. No one had ever treated her so kindly, especially a man.

"You're sure it won't be an inconvenience Edmond?"

"Not at all." he assured her.

They went down the hall again and stopped at the secretary's desk.

"I will not be available until Monday Lori, so if anything important comes up contact Gerald and he'll handle it."

"Yes Mr. Wallace," she answered.

With that he took a hold of Maggie's arm and led her to the exit door. Lori watched as they made their way toward the exit and out the door.

"I wonder who she is?" she asked the other secretary, an older woman.

"I don't know but I'll bet we see a lot of her from now on. Did you see the gleam in his eyes?"

Lori started typing and was very upset at the comment.

"Don't be silly, she's probably just a friend and nothing more."

"Maybe Lori, but I've never seen him look at any of us the way he was looking at her. Mark my words; there will be a lot of broken hearts around here if she stays.

Ж

Since the meeting of the board wasn't scheduled until one-thirty in the afternoon, Jake went to a nearby restaurant and had breakfast. It was nice to just relax a bit and read the paper. At the specified time he took a seat in the chambers and waited for the hearing to begin.

He had been sitting patiently listening to the board members as they discussed the pros and cons of each proposed method of redoing the highway at Thistle. He took notes as each item, such as cost, time and labor, were brought to light. Finally, having become impatient with the slowness of the process, he stood up and addressed the panel.

"Excuse me. Excuse me." he said.

Every member of the board looked up in surprise that someone would interrupt the proceedings. The board chairman addressed his comments to Jake.

"I'm sorry sir but you are disrupting these proceedings."

"Well maybe I am," answered Jake," but doesn't the public have a say in this matter?"

"Who are you and what is your concern here?"

Before Jake could answer the question, Mr. Wentz spoke up.

"This gentleman is Mr. Ritter who owns the property adjacent to the present highway that runs through Thistle. It seems he's just as impatient and impolite today as he was at our first meeting in Thistle."

"You bet I'm impatient," answered Jake. "I've been sitting here for over an hour now, listening to a lot of statistics and numbers and not once have you been concerned about the people involved in your decision."

The chairman banged his gavel on the desk and addressed Jake once again.

"If you'll be patient for just a few minutes longer Mr. Ritter, we're about to open this discussion to the public. So if you will just sit down and be quiet we'll get on with it."

Jake sat down but kept staring at Wentz who was sitting there with that half grin on his face. Oh how he disliked that man. The chairman spoke once again.

"If there are no objections from the panel we'll throw the discussion open to any interested party in this matter."

"I have no objection to the motion," replied Mr. Wentz. "However, I feel a short recess would be advantageous at this time as we have been in session for over an hour now."

"So noted," replied the chairman. "There will be a fifteen minute intermission. We will convene again at three."

"Geeze," said Jake out loud, "it's a wonder there are any roads in this damn state at the pace these meetings are conducted."

The board members ignored Jake's remarks as they exited through a rear door in the hearing room. Jake made his way to the entry door where a security guard was standing.

"Say," asked Jake, "anywhere around here a guy could get a drink?"

"Yes sir, there's a coffee machine at the end of the hall."

Jake retrieved a cigar from his shirt pocket as he answered.

"Well, I had something a little stronger in mind."

"Sorry sir," came the reply, "there is no drinking allowed in state buildings."

Jake put a cigar into his mouth and turned to walk away as the guard grabbed him by the arm.

"There's no smoking inside the building either sir."

Jake took the cigar from his mouth and placed it back into his shirt pocket.

"I'm sure glad I take my coffee black. I'll bet you Mormons don't allow cream and sugar in the building either."

Having said that, he continued down the hallway toward the coffee machine, chuckling to himself as he walked. Standing at the table, preparing herself a cup of coffee, was a middle aged woman. She observed Jake as he too found a cup and poured himself some coffee. She waited until he finished his chore.

"Are you always in that much of a hurry?" she asked.

Jake straightened up and looked in her direction. He was pleasantly surprised to see this pretty lady asking him a question.

"I beg your pardon," he asked, "are you talking to me?"

"Well, I hate to bring up the obvious, but we're the only ones here," she quipped.

Jake took a sip of coffee as he leaned back onto the table edge. He wasn't sure if he wanted to verbally confront this quick witted lady. For the first time in his life, he was lost for words but he admired her spunk and frankness. He looked her up and down as he gathered his composure.

"Do you make a habit of just walking up to strange men and asking questions?"

"All the time," she was quick to answer. "I'm a reporter for the Salt Lake City Bee."

"Well," quipped Jake," it must not be a very newsy day if you're asking me questions."

"Oh, I don't know," she answered. "I think there's a story to be told in every person."

"So you think I'm a story waiting to happen?"

"Well, if you keep persisting on badgering the committee in there, you're just wasting your time. It's probably safe to say you're probably wasting your time anyway."

"What do you mean by that?" Jake asked.

She walked over to the trash can and deposited her empty cup into it. Then she walked over to Jake and stood right in front of him.

"I could be wrong, Mr. Ritter, but nine times out of ten the decisions in these matters have been made long before these hearings are open to the public."

That really upset Jake.

"Well then why even hold the hearings at all if it's all cut and dried?" he asked.

"Well, my inside sources tell me that, by law, they are required to hold open hearings so the public has a chance to give their input. Then, when the decision is finally made, the public feels they had a part in the decision."

From down the hall came the announcement for all concerned parties to return to chambers as the hearing was about to commence once again.

"Thank you for the information Miss......"

"I'm Patty Webb." she said as she extended her hand for him to shake. "That is Miss Patty Webb."

"I'm Jack Ritter," he answered as he shook her hand.

"I know," she answered.

Together, they made their way back to the chambers.

"Say," he asked. "How's about I buy you a drink after this so called hearing? I think I'm going to need one."

She smiled at him.

"Hum, sounds like a good idea to me but why don't you join me at my place? They don't sell liquor over the counter here."

"Oh that's right," Jake quipped. "I forgot we're in the land of Not. So I'll meet you here after the hearing then."

Jake returned to his chair as the committee seated themselves once again. He glanced over to where Patti was sitting. She was sitting there with her legs crossed as she smiled at him. He took the opportunity to look her over pretty well and wondered to himself if she was for real? Oh well, he thought, at least the trip might not be a total waste of time.

Ж

Maggie and Edmond were on their way to visit Aunt Edna and Maggie's sisters and Maggie was very nervous. Edmond was quick to sense her anxiety.

"Are you going to be alright Maggie?" he asked.

"I'll be alright Edmond, I'm just nervous about seeing Aunt Edna. I haven't seen her for at least ten years. She and my mother never got along and nobody ever told us why but she did go to their funeral and take the kids back with her and I'm so grateful for that."

"What is your Aunt's last name? I'm in a familiar area here on this street."

"Her name is Edna Baylor Firestone and I think she's lived here all her adult life."

Edmond smiled as he spoke.

"What a small world this is Maggie. I've had some business dealings with her over the years. She's a great lady and quite a humanitarian, if I may say so.

Edmond pulled the car into a driveway and came to a stop at the large gate at the entrance and rolled down his window. A man's voice came over the loudspeaker.

"May I help you?"

"Yes," answered Edmond. "Mrs. Firestone's niece is here to see her aunt. I believe she is expected."

There was a buzzing sound as the gate began to swing open.

"Please drive to the front of the house where someone will greet you and show you into the house. Mrs. Firestone is expecting you."

Edmond started up the long, tree lined, driveway. Maggie sat in awe at the sight and was overwhelmed when the house came into view. It was a three story mansion surrounded by huge lawns and beautiful gardens; all were groomed perfectly.

"Now I'm really scared," she said.

Edmond reached over and clasped her hand and gave it a gentle squeeze as he reassured her everything would be fine.

"You're very fortunate to have Edna as your aunt. She's always very fair in matters and is a good listener and she'll expect nothing less from you."

The butler was waiting for them at the front entrance of the house. He approached the car as it came to a stop and opened the door on Maggie's side and offered his hand to her as she exited. She had never had that kind of treatment before but was taking it all in as it happened. Edmond got out on his side of the car and joined them at the entrance where he immediately took her hand in his to give a little support.

"If you'll please follow me onto the terrace, I'll inform Mrs. Firestone of your arrival."

Edmond and Maggie both sat down in lounge chairs and waited for Edna to make her entrance. Maggie looked around at the surroundings, hoping to get a glimpse of her sisters but no one was in sight. She thought, however, that she heard children laughing off at a distance. There was no chance to investigate as her Aunt Edna entered the terrace from a room with a sliding glass door. She walked forward to greet her guests and, as she reached Maggie, pulled her close and hugged her. With that gesture, all the anxiety that was pent up in Maggie quickly disappeared.

As they parted Maggie introduced Edmond to her.

"Edmond, this is my Aunt Edna. Aunt Edna, this is my friend Edmond Wallace from Salt Lake City. He was gracious enough to bring me here to see you."

She extended her hand toward Edmond and he shook hands with her as she studied him very closely.

"Do we know each other Mr. Wallace?" she asked.

"I'm afraid we do Mrs. Firestone," he replied. "I served as the chairman of your charity drive two years ago."

"Of course," she acknowledged. "You did such a splendid job for us and it turned out to be the most successful event so far."

"You're very kind, Mrs. Firestone, but I had a lot of great people working with me and your generosity spoke for itself."

"Please call me Edna. If you are going to be a friend of my niece's we can't be so formal."

They all sat at a patio table as lunch was being served by the staff.

"It's a pleasant surprise to see you again Edmond," she exclaimed. "We must get together more often and do other projects for our city."

"Thank you very much. I would love to participate in any venture you have in mind."

As they ate, they chatted about different things. Finally Maggie could stand it no longer and just had to ask about her sisters.

"Aunt Edna, are my sisters here at the house?"

"Yes they are my dear. They are playing in the swimming pool on the other side of the house. I didn't tell them you were coming because, if something came up and you couldn't make it, they wouldn't be disappointed. Besides, I thought we should talk in private before you see them, if that's alright?"

Maggie looked at Edmond as she answered, remembering what he had told her about her aunt.

"Of course it's alright Aunt Edna. I'm just overanxious I guess." she replied.

They continued to just chatter as they ate, talking about Edmond's company and the war effort and it's drawing to a close in Germany. Edna asked a few questions about Maggie's life the past two years and was pleased to learn Maggie had a business to run. After all had finished eating, Edna addressed both of her guests as she stood up.

"Edmond, would you be so kind as to excuse Maggie and me for a spell. We have some important business to attend to in the house. It shouldn't take very long. While you're waiting, Alvin would be glad to show you the stables and our fine Arabian horses or you are welcome to just sit here and read today's paper."

"Why, I'd love to see your horses. They're the talk of the state you know?"

"How kind of you to say so Edmond."

With that, Edna took Maggie by the hand and walked toward the house.

"Come along my dear," she beckoned. "We have important business to attend to and I think I've kept you waiting long enough." Hand in hand they made their way to the house where they entered a huge room that appeared to be a library. There was a large fire place made of beautifully colored stone and pictures were placed on top of the mantle. There were shelves and shelves of books in glass cases and leather furniture. Edna motioned for her to sit in the leather chair in front of the desk while she took her place behind it. Edna straightened the papers in front of her on the desk.

"Can I get you something to drink, my dear, before we start?" asked Edna.

"No Aunty, I feel just fine, thank you."

"For months now, I've wondered why a bright young girl like yourself would ever run away from home like you did. I must admit, I was very disappointed in you when I first heard that you had; however, Lottie has filled me in on what took place on that dreadful day you left home. Frankly, I don't blame you one bit and I can't tell you how shocked I am with your parents; him for treating his own children like that, and my sister for allowing it to happen."

Maggie reached for her handkerchief to wipe her eyes as she sobbed openly.

"I'm sorry we have put this burden on you Aunt Edna. It was so kind of you to take my sisters away from that terrible place and give them this beautiful place to live."

"What else could I have done Maggie? You are my flesh and blood and now I know I must help you to raise your sisters. Have you any plans for the four of you?" she asked.

Maggie straightened in her chair as she addressed the question. She knew what she said now was just as important as how she said it, so she selected her words very carefully.

"Well, here is what I have in mind. I am part owner in a café in Thistle, Utah and I am doing very well and have been putting money away so I could, one day, bring them to live with me. I don't know what else I can do. I'm all they have now so we'll just have to make the best of things."

"I admire your loyalty to your sisters and your willingness to take care of them and provide for them. I am prepared to help you realize your dreams to the point where all of you will benefit from what I have set up in your behalf. If you agree to the terms of our agreement, you'll be able to plan all of your futures."

Aunt Edna proceeded to read the documents in front of her to Maggie. There was to be a trust fund for each of the younger girls that would take effect upon their graduation from high school, but only if college was to be their next step in life. Those choosing not to further their education would be given $5,000 to be a starting point on whatever they chose to do.

As for Maggie, a bank account in her name would be set up immediately to help provide for her and her sisters to the tune of $10,000.

Aunt Edna removed her glasses and leaned back in her chair. She thought for a moment and then addressed Maggie.

"The only thing you will have to do is provide a monthly account of how the money is spent. As long as the money is used wisely you will have access to it. I just want you to be able to raise your sisters without worrying about financial matters and I want them to be able to concentrate on their studies. That seems to cover everything Maggie. Are there any questions before we join the others by the pool?"

Maggie looked down as she answered, unsure if the question she was about to ask would be taken wrong.

"You're doing so much for us and we are so very grateful, but why are you doing all this? You very seldom came to visit us in Wheaton and when you did you never stayed very long. It's like you and my mother never got along with one another."

Edna rose from her chair and walked across the room to the large window facing the garden. She stood silent for a moment and then began to talk softly. It was as though she had taken herself back in time and was reliving a moment in her life.

"Years ago two sisters lived with their parents in a small town in Iowa. Their father ran a merchandise store and each month a salesman would stop by and stay a few days to take orders from some of the businesses in town. Father was kind enough to offer our extra room for him stay in while in town.

The sisters were both in high school, the oldest a senior, the youngest a junior. The older sister became very friendly with the young man and they became very close over the months. It was all very innocent but the girl found herself falling in love with him. The younger sister became very jealous of her sister.

When the young man returned the next month, the older sister was visiting her grandmother in Cascade, Iowa for a few days. The younger sister took advantage of her absence and would sneak into the young man's room at night. When the older sister returned she was told her younger sister and the salesman had run off together and were married shortly after."

Maggie was stunned at what she was hearing. She couldn't believe her mother would do something like that to her own sister. Before she could speak, Aunt Edna continued on with the story, almost as though she had been waiting all her life to tell someone in the family what had happened so many years ago.

"In those days the oldest daughter was expected to always marry first and the younger daughters of the family were expected to honor that code. Your mother, by not honoring it, placed me in a shameful position. It was so hard to bear, with friends gossiping about it and all the snickering going on when people passed you on the street. Finally, I could stand it no longer and asked my father to let me finish my schooling in a private girl's school in Chicago, Illinois. He agreed and

I spent one year there before attending Chicago University.

Maggie stood up and walked over to her aunt and put her arm around her shoulder.

"I'm so very sorry Aunt Edna. I had no idea anything like that took place. I can see now why you didn't come to see us very often."

"To finish my story and bring you up to date on how I reached this point in my life, I'll just say this. When I was attending college I met the man who was to be my husband. I still hadn't fully recovered from my sister's doings so I hadn't dated in a long time. I guess I was afraid of losing someone else and I didn't want to go through that again. I think Franklin recognized my dilemma and so was very gentle with my feelings. I became Mrs. Franklin Firestone the day after he graduated from college. Two years later he formed his own company and we prospered. He passed away a few years ago and now I am left with all this wealth and property. We truly loved one another and I have missed him terribly."

"Did you not have children of your own?" asked Maggie.

"Somehow we never got around to making a family of our own. He was always pushing himself to succeed, mostly for me I think, and having children would have just prolonged his mission."

"Didn't you want children either?"

Edna walked over to her chair and sat down, pondering Maggie's question.

"It bothered me at first and then when your parents had your brothers and then you and then later your three sisters, I guess that was satisfaction enough. You see, deep down I always loved your father and I guess I just pretended all of you were mine."

"So that's why you took them with you after my parents died and brought them here to live with you."

"Yes and I've been enjoying our time together ever since, almost as though they were mine."

"I can't thank you enough for watching over them and for what you are proposing to do in our behalf."

"Well, enough about me my dear. Come here and sign these papers and our business will be complete. Poor Mr. Wallace is probably bored to tears by now but I think he will understand."

Maggie signed the agreements and together they went outside

and walked across the lawn toward the swimming pool where the girls were having a great time. To their surprise, Edmond had joined them poolside and appeared to be having as much fun as the girls. As they approached the pool area Lottie spotted Maggie and screamed delightfully. She exited the pool and raced toward Maggie as Tracy and Kim joined in the excitement. Maggie couldn't contain her emotions any longer and began running toward her sisters. They ran into each other on the grassy area by the pool and all fell down, hugging and kissing one another. They were laughing and crying at the same time as Edna and Edmond watched in amazement, feeling all their joy.

"Why don't you girls get your towels and go inside and change into your clothes. When you come back we'll talk about the things you'll do for the rest of the day", ordered Edna.

The girls ran to the house holding hands and laughing all the way. Maggie hadn't seen her sisters that happy, ever. The three adults made their way back to the patio, where refreshments were being served, and sat down.

"Well," asked Edna, "What are your plans for the rest of the day Edmond?"

Maggie answered before he could say anything.

"Oh, I think I've imposed enough on Mr. Wallace today. Besides, he has a business to run and I've got to get back to Thistle."

"Nonsense." said Edmond. "I took the day off so I could have a three day weekend and I want to spend the time to show you and the girls a good time. After all, I think it's about time all of you had fun together again. What do you say?"

Edna didn't give Maggie a chance to answer as she walked over to Edmond.

"Just what do you have in mind to do Edmond?"

"Well, I thought I'd give the girls a choice of going swimming at Saltair in the salt water or going to Lagoon and do all the rides, and it's my treat."

"Well the girls must be waterlogged by now so I think they'll be for going on some fun rides at Lagoon," suggested Edna.

"What's Lagoon?" asked Maggie.

"Oh, it's a play land park in Ogden. It'll be fun Maggie," said

Edmond. "We'll drive back to Salt Lake, park downtown and ride the Bamberger train to Lagoon. It lets you off right at the entrance. We'll catch the last train back at about six and we can get back here at about seven, if that's alright with you Edna?"

"Of course it's alright with me Edmond. What do you say Maggie, sound like fun to you?"

"It sounds like a lot of fun and I know the girls will love doing something like this. We never had anything like this in Wheaton."

"It's settled then," said Edmond.

The girls returned to the patio dressed in their new summer dresses and were thrilled to learn about the plans for the rest of the day. Edna walked arm and arm with Maggie to Edmond's car as he and the girls went ahead and piled in. Edna whispered to Maggie.

"Mr. Wallace is quite the eligible bachelor you know. I'm glad you two are friends."

"Aunt Edna, what are you trying to say?" she giggled.

"These are hard times my dear, you don't want the good ones to get away."

Maggie kissed Edna on the cheek and thanked her for everything.

"We'll see you tonight Aunt Edna."

They all waved goodbye as Edmond drove down the driveway to the street.

Chapter Seven

Jake took his seat once again as the panel seated themselves at their tables. The panel consisted of five members now, sitting there like little puppets, without strings, as the head honcho in the middle opened the proceedings.

"The meeting will now come to order. This segment of the meeting will be open to the public for their input on the matter concerning a new highway consideration at the town of Thistle. Does anyone wish to speak, and if so, will you please approach the microphone in the center aisle?"

With that invitation, Jake stood up and stood before the microphone and was about to make his presentation to the board. Before he could say anything he heard a voice from the main table to state his name and the nature of his business.

"My name is Jake Ritter and I own all the businesses that make up the place called Thistle. I am here to state my position on the pending proposals for a new highway through that section."

"Are you familiar with all the proposals on the table concerning this matter?"

"Yes, I have been briefed by your Mr. Wentz."

"Would you please state your position in the matter and tell this committee which proposal you are in favor of."

"Well one of your proposals is out of the question. Proposal 'A' would take half my parking lot and besides, Wentz says, after reviewing it, it would be impossible to expand the road on the east side of the existing road because the railroad owns that land as their right of way."

All the board members were studying the proposals in front of them on the desk.

"You're absolutely correct on that point. You must realize Mr. Ritter, if we approve this plan we will be taking a twenty foot wide, half mile section that fronts two of your businesses. Of course you will be compensated for the property taken and at a fair price."

"I can't afford to lose that much frontage at any price," he yelled back.

The gavel hit the table hard as the commissioner tried to control Jakes outburst.

"Mr. Ritter, you'll have to control your temper if you wish to be a part of this hearing. I suggest you state your thoughts on this question and then let us decide which plan we are going to adopt. One more outburst and I'll have security remove you from these hearings. Is that understood Mr. Ritter?"

"Yes, I understand," came Jakes reply.

"We can see you are not in favor of Plan 'A' because of the loss of frontage property. That leaves Plan 'B' and Mr. Wentz will read aloud the details of this plan for the record."

Wentz shuffled the papers in front of him. When he came to the plan to be read, he looked over the paper directly at Jake and smiled.

"Plan 'B' is as follows. The new highway would start at the north end of the canyon and go south for two miles, bypassing the establishments known as Thistle. There would take into consideration an 'on' and 'off' ramp at both the north and south ends of the project as to enable traffic, wishing to use the facilities in Thistle, to exit and return to the main highway."

Jake was yelling his objections again.

"You know damn well if you bypass Thistle my business will go under."

Wentz addressed the board in a smug and condescending manner.

"I want it on the record that this outburst by Mr. Ritter is exactly his demeanor when I visited him in Thistle."

Jake made his way down to the railing that separated the visitors from the panel. He was ranting and raving all the way.

"You're all just a bunch of crooks who don't give a damn about the livelihood of the citizens."

He looked over at Wentz who was smiling and really enjoying Jakes loss of temper. Seeing how smug Wentz was, Jake leaped over the railing and made a lunge for him but was intercepted by a security guard and thrown to the floor. The rap of the gavel sounded over and over again with a call to order. When order was restored the guard was instructed to remand Jake to the police for arrest on disrupting a legal meeting in a government office. As they escorted Jake from the meeting they walked right by Sally who was standing by the door. As they walked by, she spoke.

"I told you how it would go."

"You were right." yelled Jake. "They made up their minds long before this meeting took place."

As they ushered him from the room he was still calling them crooks.

Jake was booked into the city jail for a misdemeanor and was given a choice by the judge of paying a fine of five hundred dollars or five days in jail. He paid the fine and was released. After retrieving his belongings he made his way to the entrance to the police station. As he reached the outside stairs he was met by Sally, who was sitting on the bench outside waiting for him. She walked toward him and then joined in as he walked down the street.

"Well, Mr. Rittter," she began, "How was your stay in our wonderful jail? You sure made the counsel sit up and take notice. They approved Plan B by a unanimous vote which almost puts you out of business."

Jake was really upset and not in the mood for her joking.

"What are you doing here anyway, come by to say "I told you so?"

"Boy, you really are upset," she answered. "Don't blame me if you have a short fuse."

"Alright, I apologize. But you have to understand this will destroy everything I've worked for these past few years. Everything I dreamed of having will be lost if they bypass Thistle."

She felt his sorrow now and was upset with herself for making light of his situation.

"How about we go over to my place and I fix my famous spaghetti and have a little wine with it?"

"The food sounds great but I'm really interested in something a little stronger than wine at the moment."

"No problem," she answered. "I'll break into my private stock. I've been waiting for a moment like this to give it a try."

"Well, if you don't have a car we're going to have to call a cab because I'm going back to Thistle on the train."

"You won't get the next train to Thistle until morning and we won't need a cab because I have an apartment two blocks from here and the walk will do us good."

They walked arm in arm down the street and the more they talked the less uptight he became.

"Do you always have all the answers?" asked Jake.

"Not always but I like to think I can come close."

As they arrived at the entrance to the apartment complex Jake turned and faced her at the steps.

"Kind of dangerous bringing men to your apartment, who you don't know, isn't it?" asked Jake.

They entered the building as she answered his question. "Ordinarily yes, but I know you pretty well from the records from the highway department. They run a file on all concerned citizens wanting a say in their operations so they know who they are dealing with. As a reporter, I have limited access to those files as a matter of public records so I took the time to read your file."

"Boy, is nothing private any more?" Jake answered.

They came to her door and she unlocked it and they entered. Seemed like a nice quiet place with the usual furniture and surroundings.

"Make yourself at home while I get dinner on the stove."

Jake walked over to the mantle which was lined with many photos of Sally and various people. Jake noticed most of the photos were taken of the military in what appeared to be war zones.

"You've got quite a collection of memories here on the mantle."

"All those on the mantle were taken when I was assigned to the general staff at General Eisenhower's command post in Europe in 1944. I worked for U.P.I. then."

Jake's curiosity got the better of him as he scanned the photos.

"How does someone, who is a top reporter for United Press International, end up as a reporter for the Salt Lake City Bee covering the going's on of the highway department, if you don't mind my asking?"

Sally came into the living room from the kitchen and stood by Jake as she pointed out the various pictures and who was in them. Jake was really impressed with a group photo that included Sally, high ranking officers and General Eisenhower. She handed him a glass of whisky.

"You're in with some really high brass in this one."

"Funny you should notice that one out of all of these. I call it "My ticket home" picture."

"I don't get it."

"Well you see, I am standing by General Wilby, whom I was assigned to cover during the war. To make a long story short, I guess I covered him too well and when his wife found out she went to Ike with it. Needless to say, U.P.I. called me back to the states. After a lengthy lecture on morals and good journalism I was let go. The 'Bee' was looking for a reporter and I was looking for a job and 'wall'ah', here I am."

With that, she faced him and put her arms around him. Jake put his arms around her and looked into her eyes.

"So they lectured on what not to do with those you are doing a story on?"

"Yep."

She kissed Jake on the mouth and he returned the favor.

I'm going to go in and turn off the burners for awhile, if you don't mind?"

"You haven't learned a thing they were telling you, have you?"

"No," she answered, "I guess I never will."

ЖК

Edmond drove to the front of Aunt Edna's house and stopped. All the girls, including Maggie, were sound asleep. They had had a very tiring day at Lagoon in Ogden. After they had left Edna's, Edmond drove all of them to Salt Lake City where he parked the car in a lot. From there they boarded the Bamburger train which took them to the entrance of Lagoon. They spent all day on the rides, the fun house and eating cotton candy and candied apples. They all laughed and played and Edmond told Maggie they all deserved some happiness, including her. He gently moved Maggie's arm to wake her up.

"I hate to bother you sleeping beauties but we're at your aunt's house."

"Oh," said Maggie, "Come on girls, we're home."

Edmond got out of the car and went around to the passenger side and opened both doors. Maggie woke Lottie , who got out of the car. Maggie picked up Kim, who was still asleep, while Edmond carried Tracy. Edna met them at the door and showed them to the girls' bedrooms. Maggie kissed them goodnight and followed Edmond and Edna downstairs.

"Do you wish to stay here tonight?" asked Edna.

Edmond and Maggie looked at one another without saying anything.

"Well, if the two of you don't mind, I think the night is still young and I know a nice place we can get a cup of coffee," said Edwin.

"Sounds good to me," said Maggie. "That's if you don't mind Aunt Edna?"

Edna took them both by the hand and walked them to the front door, talking as they walked.

"Far be it from an old lady to stand in the way of a relationship. You're no longer a child Maggie and I know you'll make the right decisions. As for you Edmond, I can't think of a finer person I'd want to watch over my niece. Go on now and have a grand time together."

Maggie thanked Edna, said goodnight and kissed her on the cheek and left with Edmond. He thanked Edna for a wonderful day.

"I hope to see you often. Come back when you can."

They walked to the car and Edmond opened the door for her and then went around to the driver's side and got in. They exited the driveway and went north toward Salt Lake. He was glad he had Maggie all to himself for awhile as they hadn't had a chance to visit with one another.

"Finally," he said. "I've wanted to be alone with you all day so we could get to know each other better."

I know and it was so gracious of you to allow me to take care of my family matters today. How can I make it up to you? I'll need to go back to Thistle soon but we still have the rest of this evening if you like."

"Well, if you don't mind, I'd like to show you my house and maybe have my cook, Ella, fix us a late dinner."

"Are you sure she won't mind doing that? It's past dinner you know."

"She won't mind. Ella lives on the estate with her husband and two children. Her husband, Albert, is my grounds keeper and they know they are always on call."

Maggie couldn't believe all this was happening to her, a waitress from the 'Sisters' Café in Thistle, Utah. What were the odds? She reached over and touched his arm.

"I think that's a great idea," she said smiling.

As they made their way to Edmond's home, he suddenly reached over and took her hand in his as he spoke.

"You know Maggie, I think I'm in love with you."

She looked at him and gave a little chuckle as she spoke.

"How can you say you're in love with me Edmond when you've only known me about a week now?"

"Oh no," he answered. "I've known you all my life; I just didn't find you until now."

She blushed as the car pulled up to Edmond's house.

Chapter Eight

The warm days of summer were fading away now, letting in the brisk winds of October that made the falling leaves dance through the air as they made their way down from the tree tops. Soon there would be much rain and a blanket of winter snow that would cover the ground until springtime.

Time was not an ally to Jake as events seemed to be smothering him; and to offset the discomfort of that, he began to drink more heavily. He would sit at his desk in the garage office and ponder what moves he would have to take to keep his world afloat. He could see out his window that the highway department had kept their promise of a bypass, as large earth moving machines were put into place on the cliff overlooking Thistle. He could hear Wentz's laughter ringing in his ears, reminding him of that terrible day in Salt Lake, when the vote by the department of highways took the first step to ruin the dream that was Thistle.

He went into the garage and began working on a car. A car entered the pump area outside and activated the bell system, signaling a customer was at hand. Jake had just gotten under the car he was fixing when the bell rang. You could hear his swear words clear out to the pumps as he pushed the "creeper" out from under the car. He was wiping the grease from his hands with a towel in preparation to wait on the customer. Before he could complete that task, a man walked in the garage and called his name.

"Are you in here Mr. Ritter?"

"Yea, I'm here." Jake replied. "What can I do for you mister?"

The man walked toward Jake with his arm extended as if to shake hands.

"I'm Coach Cross. Your son Josh plays baseball for us at the high school."

As soon as he heard the name, Jake turned the other way and prepared to return to his work. Coach Cross withdrew his hand, as it was evident Jake wasn't about to shake it. He approached Jake once more in an effort to make conversation, but before he could say anything, Jake began ranting.

"You've made a trip here for nothing Cross because I'm not interested in you or your team."

"Well, you don't have to be interested in those things but aren't you interested in your son's future in baseball?"

Jake turned and looked the coach right in the eyes as he spoke.

"Oh, I'm interested in my son's future alright, but it has nothing to do with baseball or you, so why don't you go back where you came from."

The coach was upset now but was determined to state his case in Josh's behalf as he took another step toward Jake, who was leaning up against the work bench with his arms folded, listening.

"Your son has a great chance to play in the big leagues some day because he's that good. I can't believe you won't allow him to follow his dream. It's an honorable profession."

Jake took a step toward the coach as he spoke.

"Honorable profession! Honorable profession! Are you kidding me? Tell me about the 'honorable' ball players, of which you were one, who gave baseball a black eye when they caused the 'Black Sox' scandal by throwing the World Series."

"Yes, I admit that happened and it was a dark day for baseball, but I was just a rookie and was not involved in that in any way."

"Maybe so, Cross, but now that you don't play any more, you've taken on the job of finding boys who play baseball and feeding them with ideas of grandeur in professional baseball."

Jake was standing right in front of the coach's face as he continued speaking.

"Tell me the truth Cross, do you ever bring it to those boys attention about how many hopeful youngsters actually make it to the 'Big Leagues'? Along the way in their training, during high school, do you ever encourage them to be just as interested in some other vocation, just in case they don't turn out to be as gifted as you told them they were?"

Jake was tapping his finger against the coach's chest as he backed him out the doorway and into the gas pumps.

"Now, I may be wrong by insisting Josh learns this business, but the odds are in my favor that this is where he'll end up, so get in your car and get off my property." Jake said as he gave Cross a little shove.

The coach turned and faced Jake once more as he backed toward his car.

"I can't believe you won't let him play in this 'All Star' game. You don't know how good he is. You've never even been to one of our games."

Jake took another step toward the coach.

"Do you know why that is coach? It's because, when you have Josh playing baseball, I have to be here to run this business by myself and that may be alright during school, but it isn't alright for all star games. Now go back where you belong."

The coach got into his car and drove away as Jake returned to his work in the garage, not noticing Little Jake standing in the doorway to the office. The boy ran up the hill to the café where he took a seat by Josh.

"Guess what Pa just did to your coach?"

Josh turned and looked at his brother, who was all excited.

" Little brother, calm down. Now what's this about Coach Cross?"

Little Jake took a deep breath and began to tell the news.

"Coach came to ask Pa why he wasn't letting you play in the All-Star game and that made Pa mad. They argued for a minute and then Pa ran him off the property. Boy, was Pa ever mad.

Maggie overheard the conversation and went over to where the boys were talking. Before Josh could get out of his chair, Maggie held him by the arm and tried to calm him down.

"Hold on a minute Josh," she begged, "Let's not fly off the handle before you think things out. Your Pa is probably very upset at the moment, so I think you're better off to talk with him this evening when he's gotten over it."

Josh pulled his arm from her grasp and walked towards the door. He turned and faced them before exiting.

"You're just like he is. It's always about Pa's feelings; don't say anything that will upset Pa. Well what about my feelings and what about my life and the dreams I have. I know what I want and no one can keep me from getting it. Not him, not anybody."

With that, he walked outside and slammed the door behind him and headed toward the cabins. Shortly afterwards, Jake came in and sat at his usual place at the counter and asked for a cup of coffee. Maggie brought it over and sat it in front of him and then pretended to be doing some work at the counter in front of him.

"You know you're pretty low on Josh's list right now for the way you treated Coach Cross."

Jake was surprised that anyone knew of the incident but let it pass as it wasn't important who knew.

"So, what else is new?" he asked in a sarcastic tone of voice. "I make the decisions regarding my children and their welfare. When Josh is old enough, he can speak for himself, but until then, I call the shots."

Beth entered the café and sat next to her father at the counter. She had a worried look on her face, which Maggie noticed right away.

"What's the matter honey?" asked Maggie. "You look down and out this morning; something bothering you?"

"It's been a month since I heard from Jimmy and I'm worried the decision about his leg didn't go well and now he won't want to see me again."

Jake put his arm around her to console her as he attempted to reason with her.

"Look sweetheart," he began. "The army has a way of doing things in their own time. Besides, if something has gone wrong, you would have known by now. Now, Jimmy was in the hospital recovering from some sort of wounds he received in battle and those don't heal overnight."

Beth had tears in her eyes as she answered.

"I know that Pa, but if he would just write and tell me what's going on so I don't worry. I don't know if he's lost his leg or if he's alright and is coming home or anything. I just hurt so much inside."

Maggie put her hand on Beth's arm and handed her a handkerchief to dry her eyes and blow her nose.

Beth dried her eyes and thanked Maggie and her Pa for listening to her and then slid down from the chair.

"I'm going to the cabin and lay down for awhile. Maybe there will be a letter from Jimmy in today's mail delivery." she said as she walked towards the door.

Jake turned in his chair and yelled to her.

"Well, I wouldn't get my hopes up if I were you. He told you he wouldn't write again because he was coming home soon."

Maggie reached over and grabbed Jakes arm and turned him back around in his chair. She was visibly upset with him.

"Why are you telling her that? You know she's worried to death about Jimmy. My God Jake, don't you have any compassion for anyone?"

Jake pulled his arm back from her grasp and as he did so, Maggie walked away in total disgust. He sensed how she felt but couldn't let the subject go.

"You girls are all alike." he yelled to her. "You don't know how to face up to things when things go wrong."

She had heard enough from Jake; and as she spun around she took off her apron and walked back toward him, glaring at him all the way. The customers in the café couldn't help but overhear what was going on between them; and they just sat in silence and watched as she threw the apron at him when she reached the counter. Defending himself, he spilled his coffee.

"Jake, you're nothing but a self-centered loser, who cares nothing about other peoples' feelings or needs. If what your children feel goes against your wants for your precious Thistle, then you have to squash their dreams. You know why that is Jake? Because you use people to fulfill your own needs. You need me and the kids to keep this place running. Now, they are your kids and I can't do anything about them, but I sure as Hell can tell you to find somebody else to run this place. I quit!"

With that being said, she turned and went to the back room with Jake yelling at her all the time.

"Go ahead and quit Maggie. You don't have anywhere else to go. What are you going to do, run crying to Edmond in Salt Lake in the hopes he will feel sorry for you and take you in?"

Hearing what Jake had just said, she returned to the counter and stood before him. She talked in a hushed tone of voice, almost as though she wanted him to hear every word she had to say.

"For your information Jake, Edmond and I are going to be married soon and the girls and I will be living in Salt Lake. He wanted to get married right away but I told him I couldn't just walk out on you and the café. I can see now that was a mistake because you only think about yourself. I'll be making arrangements with Edmond to come and get me and my belongings within the next few days."

Jake stood up and pointed towards the door.

"Good enough. Now get out of here and don't come back. Who needs you anyway? Any one of the help could do the job you're doing. Go on, get out of here", Jake shouted.

Maggie grabbed her purse from behind the counter and walked toward the door. She had a few parting words of her own on her way out.

"Well they won't have to know much because this place will be closing down in a few weeks as the state bypasses your precious little Thistle. The only one looking for a place to go will be you, so here's a suggestion for you. Go to Hell."

She slammed the door behind her and ran toward the cabins, crying, wondering how all of this could have happened so soon. She entered the cabin where she found Beth reading the last letter she received from Jimmy. Maggie went directly to her bed and sat there crying.

Beth went to her and put her arm around her.

"What's the matter Maggie? Why are you crying?"

Maggie placed her handkerchief to her eyes and stopped crying, not wanting to upset Beth. She reached over and placed her hands on Beth's hands.

"Look honey, I'm going to be leaving soon. I'll be living in Salt Lake with my sisters and Edmond. He has asked me to marry him and I've decided it is the best thing to do under the circumstances. I hate leaving you and the boys, but your father wants me out of here as soon as possible."

"Oh no Maggie." she pleaded. "I don't want to be here if you're not here. I'm afraid, what with Pa drinking so much now and his temper. Please take me with you Maggie, please."

Maggie embraced her as they were both crying now, consoling one another and Maggie trying to think of something to say. Finally they separated and Maggie placed her hands on Beth's shoulders as she spoke.

"Look honey, there's no way your Pa is going to let me take you away from here. You're just going to have to face what's coming and try to give your Pa as much help as you can."

"You ran away from your father. You didn't stay and try to help him."

Maggie turned away, for she knew Beth was right about that situation. She had set a bad example for the children and she was embarrassed.

"Yes I did Beth and I've regretted doing that ever since. But it is something I can't change now. You have time to sort things out and to make the right decisions. You've got to stay with your family, so Jimmy knows where to find you. He'll be home soon and then you can make a new life for yourself, if that's what you want."

Beth buried her face in her hands as she spoke.

"All this wouldn't have happened if we only would have kept going to California like Pa promised when we left Wheaton."

"Maybe so Beth, but then, you never would have seen Jimmy and you wouldn't be waiting for him now."

Her words seemed to comfort Beth and, looking at the situation that way, she knew what she had to do, no matter what the circumstances.

"Thank you Maggie for being such a good friend and for showing me what I need to do until Jimmy returns. I know you have to go and be with Edmond and your sisters and I am happy for you."

"Thank you Beth. Where's Little Jake? I haven't seen him all day?"

Before she could answer, there was a knock on the door and she heard Josh's voice asking if he could come in.

As he opened the door, Maggie could see the rain drops beginning to fall on the porch. The rolling sound of thunder echoed down through the canyon walls and the sky had turned a slate black beyond the cliffs.

"Have either of you seen Little Jake lately?" asked Josh.

"Yes." said Beth. "His Indian friend, Chadego, came by with his newly acquired horse and they went for a ride to their hang out in the cliffs. Why?"

There's a terrible storm brewing out there. I'm going to have a talk with Pa, then I'll go and get him and bring him home, so don't worry."

"What are you going to talk to Jake about Josh?" Maggie asked.

It's about school next year. I want to change schools and go live in Spanish Fork with Coach Cross's brother."

"Well, you do what you want Josh, but I can tell you this is not a good time to talk to your Pa about any changes you want. He and I went at it a few minutes ago and he told me to pack up and get out."

"What? What's wrong with him Maggie?"

"His world is coming down around his ears, now that the state is bypassing Thistle with the new highway. You be careful Josh, he's been drinking again and that mean streak of his has reared its ugly head."

Josh headed for the door.

"Well, he's just going to have to listen, for once, about something I want to do with my life."

Having said that, he exited the cabin and headed toward the garage. The rain had picked up now, but it didn't bother him, because he was trying to get a clear idea of just how he wanted to present his case to his father. A bolt of lightning cracked just beyond the cliffs and as he reached the office, the thunder, once again, rumbled down through the canyon as the rains picked up. He was really wet now as he entered the office.

Jake was sitting back in his chair and had his feet propped up on the desk. He was smoking a cigar and made no move to hide the bottle of whisky sitting on the desk from his son. As Josh entered, Jake reached for the bottle and proceeded to pour himself another glass of whisky.

"Well," said Jake, "if it isn't the world's greatest baseball player, or so says your wonderful Coach Cross. You know, of course, he paid me a visit today, pleading your case about playing in the All-Star game, and I threw him out on his ear. What's the matter Josh, afraid to stand on your own two feet and ask me to let you play?"

"I didn't know he was coming to see you Pa and I certainly don't need anyone to speak for me."

Jake downed the drink he had poured for himself and reached for the bottle again to refill it. He watched Josh's reaction as he poured.

"Well I guess you learn something new every day kid. What the hell do you want anyway? I don't think you came down here in the rain to talk about my drinking habits which, by the way, are none of your business."

Josh was visibly nervous for, somehow, the things he practiced to say to Jake and how he would say them, failed him now. He knew, however, this would be his only chance to make his case, so he began slowly.

"Alright Pa, here it is. My senior year is next year and I want to move to Spanish Fork so I can play where baseball scouts frequently come to watch. Coach Cross's brother is the coach there and he has agreed to let me stay with his family for the school year. So, I guess I'm asking your permission to make the move."

Surprisingly, Jake just gave Josh a simple "no" answer and then downed his drink once more.

He stood up and poured another as Josh tried to find the words he wanted to say; but, before he could react, Jake continued to speak. There was more authority in his voice this time.

"Let's save a lot of time and yelling here Josh. I've said it before and I'll say it again. Until you graduate from high school you'll do as I say because I am responsible for your actions and I can't keep an eye on you if you're a hundred miles away."

Josh didn't like Jak's reasoning on the subject and let him know his own feelings.

"You're a liar Pa and you know it. You don't want me to go because then you would have to run this place all by yourself. You want me to be a mechanic, but I say it doesn't matter what you want me to be; it's what I want to do in my life that counts."

Jake took a step towards his son, and as he did, Josh backed up a step for he saw the look in Jake's eyes. He was afraid of him now and he had never been afraid of his father until that moment.

"Well, you can slice it any way you want, you little ingrate, but you're staying here and you're going to help me run this garage."

Josh was as mad as Jake now and he retrieved the step he had taken a few minutes earlier and now stood face to face with his father. He knew this moment would be his only chance to express his true feelings to Jake, so he took it.

"I may not be the son you wanted me to be but you're definitely not the father I had in Kansas before you used all of us to fulfill your dream here in Thistle. You're a user Pa and you'll do whatever it takes to hang on to this God forsaken hole in the wall 'rest stop'. You've used all of us, and especially Maggie, but she fooled you didn't she Pa? Never in your wildest dreams did you ever think she would find someone to love her while working at the Sisters café. It's ironic, isn't it Pa, that the very person you never wanted to see come here did so through your garage? I say "good for her" and it's going to be good for me too because I'm going to Spanish Fork High School next year, with or without your permission."

From out of nowhere came the slap across Josh's face, the force of which knocked him backwards into the door.

Josh braced himself against the door as he rubbed his jaw. A tear rolled down his face as he spoke.

"I wouldn't have expected that from my father; but then you're not my father anymore. You're just a hopeless drunk who's about to lose everything and everyone you professed to love all this time."

Jake lunged at him again but Josh was ready for him this time and grabbed Jake by the shirt front and pushed him backward over the desk. Jake was so drunk he couldn't put up much resistance. Josh put his finger up to Jake's face as he spoke.

"You'll never have another chance to hit me again Pa because I'm leaving here tomorrow with Coach Cross and we're going to Spanish Fork, and there isn't anything you can do about it."

There was a loud clap of lightning that rattled the building, followed by rolling thunder, as Josh exited the building. Jake collapsed back into his chair and reached for the bottle once again. As Josh made his way toward the cliffs, he could hear the window of the office being broken by the glass Jake through it. He could see that the lightning had struck the small railroad cabin down by the tracks and it was on fire now. He wanted to help put out the fire but his main concern now was for the safety of his brother. He began running in the rain toward the dugout he knew Little Jake had carved out of the cliffs. He prayed that he and his friend, Chadego, would be there and all would be alright.

Back at the office, Jake stood at the broken window and looked out into the evening sky. It was the worst he had ever seen the sky look and the worst storm he could remember, even on the farm in Kansas. In the distance he saw the big earth moving machine parked atop the first little cliff behind Thistle. The state was using it to clear a way for the new road that was to be built.

Jake gathered up his bottle and headed out the door toward the huge machine, mumbling all the way about how unjust it all was and how ungrateful everyone was and how they all turned on him. Beth came out onto the porch as her father made his way up the cliff. She yelled at him, asking where he was going in this terrible storm. He gave no acknowledgement that he had heard her but now seemed more determined to reach the machine. Beth ran back into the house and told Maggie what she had just seen and asked what she should do.

"No time for him now Beth. Grab your coat and come on. We have to help put out the fire down by the tracks."

The storm had grown more violent now as the winds picked up and the rain began to fall all the harder. There was thunder and lightning all around Thistle now. In the hills, Josh had somehow lost his way to where he thought Little Jake's dugout was. Cold and tired and drenched to the bone, he climbed on top of a small outcropping and tried to get his bearings. Another bolt of lighting cracked off to his left which sent out roaring thunder down into the valley. He didn't get scared very often but he realized there was danger all around him now.

About a quarter mile further up the canyon, Little Jake and his friend Chadego were scurrying about trying to get onto the horse. Chadego leaped onto the horse's back and reached for his friend's hand in an effort to pull him up behind him. Babe was barking frantically as the roar of rushing water was descending down upon them from further up the canyon. Chadego kept reaching for his friend's hand as he yelled to him.

"Come on Little Jake, hurry and take my hand. I think there is a flash flood coming and we got to get out of here."

Just as Chadego grabbed his friend's hand, in an effort to pull him atop the horse, a wall of water, coming down the creek, hit Little

Jake in the back with such force that the boys lost their grip on one another and the current swept Little Jake further down the creek, which had become now a wall of raging water.

Chadego and the dog hurried after him from the side of the bank. Babe caught up with Little Jake as the water widened out momentarily in a flat spot. The dog jumped into the raging waters and swam toward the boy. As he reached his friend, Little Jake was flaying his arms around in an effort to right himself in the water. Babe grabbed the boy's sleeve in his mouth and began pulling him toward the shore where Chadego was waiting for them with outstretched arms. As he grabbed Little Jake's arm and pulled him out of the current, another huge wave struck the dog and carried him down stream at a terrific speed, where he disappeared into the darkness. The boys mounted the horse and headed for high ground where they would be safe.

The roaring waters quickly rushed down the creek bed, destroying everything in its path as it made its way toward Thistle. Tree limbs and boulders were no match for the onslaught of water that roared through the canyon. Josh could hear the oncoming torrent of water and realized he would not be safe on that outcropping where he was perched. He tried to jump to safety toward the bank of the creek but as he leaped, a wall of water smashed him against the rocks that made up the cliff. He heard the bones in his arm crack as he fought to free himself from the rocks. He momentarily sank beneath the water's surface. He was gasping for air as he freed his arm from between the rocks and, although the pain was intense, he managed to stay alert and try to find a way out of a deadly situation.

Jake, in the meantime, bottle in hand and drinking as he went, had started up the engine of the earth mover and had driven it down into the creek bed as he was unaware of any impending danger from the storm. He was waving the bottle about as he yelled obscenities into the night. Beth could see her father driving the machine as the lights of it broke through the darkness. She ran toward him, yelling for him to stop as she ran, but it was too late as the wall of water came crashing down upon him, turning the massive vehicle over on it's side as it continued to toss, at will, everything and everybody in its path at breakneck speeds.

The terror of the scene sent Beth into shock and instead of yelling "Papa, Papa", she now was now yelling "Mama, Mama" as that terrible scene of their house burning, with her mother in it, reappeared with all its horrendous scenes, leaving her to once again to relive the moment. As she relived the tragedy in her mind, she saw, for the first time, the person who was running from the house on that fateful day. Beth collapsed to the ground screaming "Papa, Papa, over and over again amidst all the thunder and lighting and the fearful sound of the flash flood.

As the high waters swept her into the expanse of the parking lot, the high water spread out and deposited her on the traffic island at the gas pumps. She had enough senses about her to grab onto one of the hoses and pull herself upright and make her way to higher ground where she fell into a heap, like a rag doll, covered with cuts and mud and blood. Her hair was matted to her wet face and as she pushed the hair from her eyes she took one last look in the direction where she last saw her father, being pushed along at a high rate of speed, tumbling over and over again amongst all the rocks and debris. She was unable to find him again in the darkness of the rushing waters.

Chapter Nine

The military hospital plane, on its way to Hill Air Force Base in Utah, had entered the storm that was plaguing the countryside around Thistle and the ride turned very bumpy as they approached the air field. There were only five military personnel aboard the plane, a crew of four and one returning soldier from the war, Private James Brandt, U.S. Army.

One of the crew members approached Jim at the rear of the plane and told him to make sure he was buckled in as turbulent weather would affect their landing. He turned to walk back to the front of the plane but stopped and turned facing Jim once again.

"Say soldier, aren't you on your way to a place called Thistle, up in the hills east of Provo?"

"Why yes I am." Jim replied. "Why do you ask?"

"Well, I hate to be the bearer of bad news Private, but a flash flood has hit the region. All reports say the place was all but destroyed and a passenger train was derailed entering the canyon. A lot of injuries I guess so the ambulance assigned to pick you up is being sent to the Provo hospital to assist in the recovery operation. You got family there?"

Jim was stunned to learn of the horrible catastrophe and he could only imagine what might have happened to Beth and her family.

"Yes, the girl I want to marry lives there with her family, along with a friend from back home in Kansas."

"We'll be landing in the next few minutes. I think, under the circumstances, you might be able to talk the ambulance crew into taking you along to Provo instead of dropping you off at the base hospital. Whatever happens buddy, I hope everything turns out alright for them and you after all you've been through."

Jim sat in silence as the plane approached the runway and touched down among swirling winds and rain. He prayed everyone would be safe and yet he knew that was a lot to ask of victims of a flash flood. He prayed as the plane taxied up to the tarmac and came to a stop.

The hatch door was opened and the electric platform was activated. A corpsman came aboard and wheeled Jim's wheelchair onto the platform and he was lowered to the ground below. The corpsman talked to Jim as he was being wheeled to the waiting ambulance.

"Sorry for the change of plans Private, but our orders have been changed because of a flash flood in the mountains east of Provo.

"Yes, I know Corporal, but you were to deliver me to Thistle where this all happened."

"Well if that's where the flood happened, I can't very well take you there. Besides, all the victims are being transferred to the hospital in Provo."

"Well then, how about a lift to the hospital?"

"We can do that soldier. We're going there first to get our instructions from "Search and Rescue". We'll get you off the ambulance at the entrance to the hospital. After that you're on your own."

"That's fair enough," Jim answered, as he sat back in the wheelchair and prepared for the journey south to Provo. The driver could hear Jim praying as they sped down the highway.

The driver of the 'Search and Rescue" ambulance backed the vehicle up to the emergency entrance of the hospital, got out and ran around to open the rear doors. Personnel from the hospital were there to meet them where they unloaded two injury victims on stretchers. Once they were taken away, Beth emerged from the vehicle and was helped to the interior of the building. She told them who she was and wanted to know if her father was there. A nurse told her they had him in room six down the hall but that he wasn't expected to make it.

Beth pulled away from the nurse and, staggering, made her way to room six. A doctor was coming out of the room as the nurse tried to stop Beth from going in. The doctor grabbed Beth by the arm.

"Who is this girl, nurse?'

"It's Mr. Ritter's daughter. They just brought her in and she insists on seeing her father."

The doctor released his grip on her arm.

"You can go on in Miss Ritter, but I've got to inform you that in all probability he won't last the night."

Beth entered the room where her father was lying on a bed with a blanket over him. He was covered with mud to the point he was almost unrecognizable. He lay there with his eyes wide open, looking at the ceiling and groning with pain. As Beth approached the side of his bed he turned and looked at her. She didn't attempt to console him, but rather, stood there with her arms at her side with tears in her eyes. Finally she spoke to him.

"You killed Mama, didn't you Papa?"

Jake turned away from her stare in disbelief.

"How can you say that Beth, I loved your mother? How can you say such a thing to me?"

"The nightmare I was having all this time finally played itself out when the trauma of seeing you taken under by the flood waters was replaced by the fire that killed Mama."

Jake was upset by what she was saying and began scolding her for thinking such a thing.

"You know those nightmares are just a figment of your

imagination and can't be relied on as truthful."

She took a step forward and stood by the bed so he would be sure to hear what she had to say.

"It was different this time Papa. This time I saw the ending to that frightening scene."

He squirmed under the blanket, very uneasy now.

"So, what did you see that would bring you to accuse me of such a thing? If you remember honey, I was on my way into town when you and your mother went out to pick wildflowers."

"Yes, you started out the driveway; believing Mama and I were on our way into the fields to pick the flowers. You turned the truck around and came back to the house and lit the fire, not knowing Mama had returned to the basement to fetch her gloves. There was so much smoke she couldn't see to find her way out and she died there. I know it was you Papa because in my nightmare I saw you running from the house, get into the truck and drive off, never looking back."

Jake turned his head and faced the wall. There were tears coming down his cheeks now as he tried to speak to his daughter. Without turning his head back to face her, he slowly began to explain what had happened. It was as though he was there again, in his childhood, with all those years working the farm; a farm he never cared about or wanted to work on; years he always believed had wasted his youth.

"I'm sorry everyday about the death of your mother, but you must believe me when I tell you, it was an accident. Yes, I burned it all to the ground Beth, because I grew tired of having to live my life doing things I really hated doing, because it was expected of me, first by my father and then, when he died, I had to keep the farm going for my mom so she would have a home. In the meantime, one by one you and your brothers came along and when your Grandma died I still was expected to keep the farm going for all of you, but I wanted something for me."

"Why did you have to burn it down Pa?"

"I tried to do it the right way, by selling everything; but your mother wouldn't hear of such a thing. So I devised my plan to destroy everything and collect the insurance on the homestead and sell the land. It was never my plan to collect any money for your mother's death."

Jake slowly turned his eyes so he could see Beth's face. He reached for her hand but she pulled it away and just stood there by the bed crying.

He was in a lot of pain now and he knew he was dying and that he was seeing his daughter for the last time on this earth.

"Did they tell you I probably won't last the night?"

Beth nodded her head up and down, assuring him she knew.

"Can you and the others forgive me? I never meant any harm sweetheart."

She became frantic when he said that and started screaming at him.

"Forgive you Pa, forgive you? I hate everything about you now for what you did. This has to be God's punishment for you and I don't care that you are dying."

With that, she spun around and raced out of the room, crying uncontrollably with her hands covering her face. She looked down the hallway and saw Maggie and Edmond sitting at the nurses' station. They stood up when they saw her, but before they could go to her to console her, the entrance door opened and there, in his wheelchair, sat Jimmy, with a blanket over his legs. Beth took one step toward him but he held up his hand in a stopping motion, so she stopped.

All the family there knew about his wounded leg but they were never told if he had to have it taken off. Slowly, he pulled the blanket from his legs and braced his hands on the side rails of the chair. Seeing him struggle with the attempt, Edmond made a move to help him but Jim motioned him back.

"Thank you anyway sir, but I'm going to have to learn to do this myself for a long time." That being said, he lifted himself up and stood on his own two feet, wobbly though it may have been.

Beth waited to see if he was able to walk, as she stood there with her hands to her face. Silently, she prayed to God he still had his legs. Standing erect, he took a step with his right leg and followed it with a step with his left leg, leaving the wheelchair behind him. Upon seeing what he had accomplished, she ran down the hallway and into his open arms where they embraced and kissed, over and over again, as the family gathered around them. Josh and Little Jake had come out of a room where they had been treated. Josh had his broken left arm set into a cast and Little Jake was treated for cuts and abrasions. They all had been told Jake wouldn't last the night as his body had been crushed beyond repair. They all knew they were lucky to be alive.

Ж

In his will, Jake had asked for permission from the state to be buried on a small knoll overlooking Thistle and they granted him that wish. Now, a week after his passing, the family and friends were gathered at his grave site on the knoll to pay their last respects to the man who, many felt, had used them to realize his own dreams and ambitions. None the less, they gathered there on this day, for whatever their reasons, to say a final farewell in their own way.

They all stood and listened as the priest gave the last blessing to their father and friend.

"Lord, we ask that you accept the soul of Jake Ritter into Your kingdom where he will dwell for all time. Forgive him his sins and raise him up into Your house with the same compassion you have always shown us. May he rest in peace, Amen."

As the priest stepped back, the casket was lowered into the grave. Little Jake was the first to step forward and drop a rose onto the casket. His heart was filled with so much sorrow, so much for a little boy to bear. He stood there crying and merely told his father goodbye. Maggie went to him and placed her hands on his shoulders and guided him back to his place with the family.

Maggie nodded to Josh, telling him it was his turn, but he shook his head no and only stood there looking at the ground beneath his feet. All were surprised that Josh had nothing to give or say to his departed father. There were no tears in his eyes.

Beth motioned for the rest of the onlookers to go before her; and as they each did what they came to do in respect for his passing, she realized, no one really knows everything about a person and that means each of us has to offer, in our own way, with the knowledge we are given, whatever that person meant to them. Finally, the last well wisher dropped their flower upon the casket.

Beth realized she was the last to stand at the gravesite and she could feel the eyes of the others watching for her to make a move. Now, without hesitation, she stepped forward to the side of the grave, opened a large bag and took from it a fully grown thistle plant she found growing in the desert. Its bloom was a brilliant purple color with little stickers on it, with green leaves and a long root that came up with the plant as she pulled it out of the ground with her bare hands. There were no tears this time as she spoke her last words to her father, aloud.

"You wanted Thistle to be your life and now you can have thistle for all eternity, wherever you're going."

Having said that, she threw the thistle plant down upon the casket where it made a loud thud.

"No Pa," she screamed, "I will never forgive you!

Epilogue

The flash flood that hit Thistle killed twenty four people; seventeen from the rail cars that were thrown off the tracks; the colored cook from the café who was standing just inside the doorway when the rushing waters crashed through the window and crushed him against the counter; three patrons who were eating in the café at the time; two railroad workers that were inside the building by the tracks when the lightning struck it, followed quickly by the onrushing waters and, of course, Jake Ritter. Search and Rescue teams recovered the body of Babe, Little Jake's dog, forty yards down stream from where he pulled the boy to safety. He got tangled up in debris and was pulled under and was drowned.

Maggie and Edmond were married in Salt Lake City a month after the flood at Thistle. Edmond welcomed her sisters into the family and treated them as his own children. Maggie and Edmond never had children of their own. They all finished their schooling and Lottie continued on in business school and opened up a gift shop directly beneath the grand ball room in Saltair, just outside Salt Lake. The resort, on the banks of the Great Salt Lake, has long since closed its doors; however, the gift shop is still there. Lottie swears she can still hear the music coming from the pavilion every now and then. The other two girls both married and had a gaggle of kids.

Josh Ritter pursued his dream of playing baseball and made it to the big leagues as a pitcher for the Saint Louis Cardinals. When no longer able to actively play the game, he and his wife lived in Salt Lake City, Utah where he managed the Salt Lake City Bees of the Pacific Coast league.

Little Jake Ritter went on to become the agent for Indian affairs for the state of Utah. His good friend Chadego, who saved his life, headed up all tribal counsels of the Ute nations. Together, these life long friends, spent their lives making sure all concerned were treated fairly and with compassion. The name 'Chadego' means 'One Who Leads'.

Beth and Jim married two months after her graduating from high school. They have four children and live in Wheaton, Kansas where they are both teachers at the grade school.

If one were to take the train from Salt Lake City to Denver, Colorado today, you would still pass through the site that was known as Thistle. If you look closely from the right side of the train windows, you can still see what buildings remain that comprised this dream that was Jake Ritter's. Of course, the town was never rebuilt after the flood, but if you look closely, you can still spot some structures sticking out of the mud with just their roofs visible. Look out the left side of the train and you'll be able to see the highway that was built by the state that bypassed the place we know as Thistle. Now, you can sit back and close your eyes as the train enters the canyon on its way up the steep grade to the top of Soldiers Summit and down the other side to Price, Utah. If you'll listen real closely you'll be able to hear the sound of the train whistle, echoing off the canyon walls; just like it's always done.

One final note about the Ritter family: The insurance money they realized from the loss of what was Thistle and the life insurance policy on Jake Ritter, was used to pay back the insurance company that insured their homestead in Wheaton, Kansas.

My story is fiction, but in reality the place called Thistle was inundated with water, around 1983, because of a huge landslide that backed up all the water in the area. Eventually, it flooded Thistle and today you can see the rooftops of those buildings that were lost. I, of course, changed the event into a flash flood to fit my story.

The End

ABOUT THE AUTHOR

Thomas Kessenich was born on January 13th, 1932 in Milwaukee, Wisconsin to Fred and Deloris Kessenich. Almost all of his youth was spent traveling around the western United States. He was joined in this venture by two brothers and a sister. They were always on the move because dad was unskilled and had to take work wherever and whenever it happened his way. Tom attended eighteen different schools in order to finish his schooling prior to high school. He graduated from Bishop Manogue High School in Reno, Nevada in 1951.

His hobbies include sports; writing poetry; art and photography. Some of his photographs of the old homesteads have been printed in magazines. He served eight years in the U.S. Air Force where he worked as a Military Policeman from 1952 until his discharge in 1960. He is currently retired living with his wife Nancy in Palisade, Colorado.